garden
pools
FOUNTAINS & WATERFALLS

By Scott Atkinson and the Editors of Sunset Books, Menlo Park, California

SUNSET BOOKS

VP, GENERAL MANAGER
Richard A. Smeby

VP, EDITORIAL DIRECTOR
Bob Doyle

DIRECTOR OF OPERATIONS
Rosann Sutherland

MARKETING MANAGER
Linda Barker

ART DIRECTOR
Vasken Guiragossian

SPECIAL SALES
Brad Moses

STAFF FOR THIS BOOK

MANAGING EDITOR
Bonnie Monte

PAGE LAYOUT
Maureen Spuhler

COPY EDITOR
Mary VanClay

PHOTO EDITOR
Scott Atkinson

PHOTO STYLIST
JoAnn Masaoka Van Atta

ILLUSTRATOR
Tracy La Rue Hohn

PRODUCTION SPECIALIST
Linda M. Bouchard

PRODUCTION ASSISTANTS
Carrie Davis, Susan Paris

PREPRESS COORDINATOR
Eligio Hernandez

PROOFREADER
Joan Erickson

INDEXER
Nanette Cardon

10 9 8 7 6 5 4 3 2 1
First Printing January 2007.
Copyright © 2007,
Sunset Publishing Corporation,
Menlo Park, CA 94025.
Fifth edition. All rights reserved, including the right
of reproduction in whole or in part in any form.
ISBN-13: 978-0-376-01227-2
ISBN-10: 0-376-01227-7
Library of Congress Control Number: 2006932479
Printed in the United States of America.

For additional copies of *Garden Pools, Fountains &
Waterfalls* or any other Sunset book, visit us at
www.sunsetbooks.com or call 1-800-526-5111.

COVER

Photo by Marcus Harpur; garden design by
Marney Hall, RHS Chelsea Flower Show 2003;
cover design by Vasken Guiragossian.

contents

READERS' NOTE: Almost any
do-it-yourself project involves a
risk of some sort. Your tools,
materials, and skills will vary, as
will the conditions at your project
site. Sunset Publishing
Corporation has made every
effort to be complete and accu-
rate in the instructions and other
content contained in this publica-
tion. However, the publisher does
not assume any responsibility or
liability for damages or losses
sustained or incurred in the
course of your project or in the
course of your use of it. Always
follow manufacturer's operating
instructions in the use of tools,
check and follow your local building codes, and observe all standard safety precautions.

THE MAGIC OF WATER

IF ANYTHING IN NATURE IS MAGIC, it must be water. The shimmer and sound of pools, fountains, and falls have cast their spell throughout history. The Chinese, and later the Japanese, perfected the balance of three basic elements: water, stone, and plants. The Romans used fountains and stair-step pools to cool hot summer nights along the Mediterranean. The English Victorians built palatial homes for goldfish, and the French spread out enormous sheets of water in front of their chateaux. Quiet and reflecting, or dancing and sparkling—water still brings both energy and old-world charm to a new-world garden.

Whether it reflects sky and clouds, a garden sculpture, or the arching branches of a nearby tree, a garden pool presents an ever-changing picture. It can be a refuge of calm, a true oasis, a wildlife haven, or a formal focal point. It can be big or small. Whatever scale or style you're after, new pool liners and hardware can help you make it happen.

Water in motion is nearly always dramatic, and a flowing fountain brings that drama to your garden. But in addition to entertaining, a fountain does more practical work. During the hot days of summer, it provides a cool retreat for you, your family, and guests. The musical sounds of a fountain also wrap the area in privacy, screening off outside noise and distractions.

Waterfalls and streams do the same thing on a larger scale. Today's flexible liners, pumps, and prefab waterfall boxes make them easier to build—just add rocks. Pondless waterfalls fit small spaces and eliminate standing water, so they're safer around small children. Want the look of a water feature without any water at all? Consider a dry creek.

If you're already an enthusiastic gardener on land, a garden pool presents a whole new world. Your yard may already be filled with flowers and shrubs, but now you can cultivate intriguing plants that won't grow on dry land, such as water lilies or lotuses.

And as a water gardener, you're not limited to plants. Goldfish or koi dimpling the surface of a still pond are a captivating sight. Raising fish—especially if you've never kept so much as a single goldfish in a glass bowl—can be very satisfying and opens up a new area of fascination for the adventurous gardener.

This book works in three ways: as inspiration, shopper's guide, and how-to primer. Each of the main subjects—pools, fountains, and waterfalls—has its own chapter, which kicks off with scores of photo ideas, joined by general planning text. Next, we offer a close-up look at all the materials—or "nuts and bolts"—that make those ideas happen. Finally, if you're so inclined, you'll find a selection of step-by-step projects. Follow these steps sequentially, or use them as a launching pad for your own creation.

Chapters on plants and fish follow, with more great photos, plant and fish encyclopedias, and down-to-earth practical pointers. Finally, we take a look at basic maintenance and repairs that can keep your new water garden in tip-top shape year-round.

Ready to start dreaming—or digging? Just read on. It's not as hard as you might think! Take your time planning, shopping, and building your water feature, and you can't go wrong. After you're done, you'll wonder how you ever lived without it. You'll also be the latest in a long line of people, stretching back to ancient times, who have happily surrendered to water's spell.

garden
pools

WHAT'S YOUR PERFECT POOL? IT MIGHT BE AS TINY AS
A TUB OR BIG ENOUGH FOR WATER LILIES AND FRISKY
FISH. MAKE IT A FORMAL SQUARE OR CIRCLE, OR PER-
HAPS A NATURAL SHAPE TUCKED AMID LUSH PLANT-
INGS. CONSIDER ADDING A FOUNTAIN, WATERFALL, OR
OTHER AMENITIES. TODAY'S LINERS AND HARDWARE
MAKE POOL BUILDING A SNAP.

STARTING SMALL

WATER IN SMALL MEASURES SERVES A SOOTHING PUR-POSE IN A GARDEN, WITHOUT ENTAILING MUCH EFFORT OR EXPENSE. Let the pool showcase a changing arrangement of container plants as seasonal blooms appear, or start a tiny tub garden (see page 117). Or accent the pool by placing a glass float or colorful flower on the water's surface. The simplest "decoration" of all is to keep the water sparklingly clear and let birds play in it.

If you'd like to start small, you can pick up tiny decorative pools at garden-supply and statuary stores.

Innovative garden decorators have also demonstrated that nearly any container capable of holding water can—with suitable sealing and placement—become an attractive accent pool. Add your own ideas to the following list: bonsai bowls, terra-cotta planters, wine barrels, industrial drums, claw-foot bathtubs, laundry basins, livestock troughs, glazed ceramic urns. Check your local masonry yard for stones and boulders that have natural bowl formations. Scout around for that chipped enamel sink, rusty wheelbarrow, or galvanized bucket. Leave the basin in its rough state or paint it, tile it, or line it with a mosaic of pebbles, seashells, or whatever you have available.

Want to shape a small accent pool yourself? Consider free-form concrete—troweled, colored, and textured to resemble a water pocket in native stone. Waterproofed lumber or marine-grade plywood can also fill the bill. For pointers, see pages 40–41.

A galvanized water trough, meant for cows, takes on new life as a portable lily pond. Try a seasonal tub garden wherever you like, then simply drain it and move it to another spot.

This simple, unplumbed water feature forms a visual mantra, guiding the viewer's thoughts away from external hubbub and inward toward petals floating in the glass bowl.

ABOVE: An artful bowl of water lilies seems to float above a rosy cloud of sedum. TOP RIGHT INSET: Moss-encrusted boulders with natural depressions hold water and look like they've been there forever.

SETTING A STYLE

POOLS CAN BE FORMAL OR INFORMAL. Having trouble figuring out which approach is best? Take a cue from your house and yard. The most successful pools echo the shapes and style of their surroundings. If you're placing your new water garden among formal beds and walkways, make it formal as well. If the surroundings are more casual, treat the pool that way, too. Here's a closer look at your options.

Going Formal

In a Victorian garden, the pool was a generous circle, oval, or rectangle, slightly raised, set in the center of an area, and surrounded by spacious walks so that it could be viewed from every side.

Though few of us have that much space these days, if you build a pool of concrete, brick, stone, or tile in a simple geometric shape, you'll succeed in

ABOVE: For a pool that says "formal," concrete is often the material of choice. In this graceful design, white concrete steps join grass-covered tiers and form soft waterfalls.

recalling the old style. Typical shapes are circles, ovals, squares, rectangles, and hexagons. They can be scaled up or down to fit the available space and harmonize with the surroundings. Fountains and splash sculpture are characteristic accessories.

Formal pools may be raised above ground level, semi-raised, or sunken, depending on the site and the border effect you wish. A raised pool requires the most effort and materials but provides surfaces for sitting and sunning, as well as for container plants and decorations. Edgings are usually geometrically shaped masonry or smooth concrete, gravel, or grass.

Often the pool is carefully located to be a focal point; it may line up with other prominent elements along a visual axis. Generally, less space is devoted to plants than in an informal water garden. What plants there are usually have neat shapes, either because they grow that way or because they've been carefully pruned or trained.

Gaining patina with age, this Mediterranean-style courtyard centers on a vibrant tiled pool and fountain. The matching surround blends terra-cotta tile squares and diagonally set blue accents.

A raised pool becomes a central garden structure and encourages one to linger on its edges. Here, native Southwest plants and stone soften the formal style.

Back to Nature

A naturalistic pool is almost any body of water without square corners, perpendicular walls, or man-made edges in sight. It might have native stone and soil close around it, along with plants common to the area in which you live. Most informal pools are sunken; some are semiraised.

Beyond that, the choices are as wide-ranging as the designs are beautiful. Yours could be an alpine pool, a willow-lined pond, a tiny spring in some desert oasis, or a water retreat modeled after one you remember from a vacation. Japanese gardens are an excellent source of natural ideas and techniques.

In the past, most natural pools were hand-packed shells of clay or concrete; today, do-it-yourselfers opt for flexible pool liners or rigid shells (see pages 26–29). It's the border that counts: Typically, edges are rimmed with lush plantings or stone, soil, and other materials that soften or hide the edges.

Unlike formal pools, informal designs fit comfortably in limited spaces. They are also more forgiving of improvised, irregular border treatments. Thinking of building a pool yourself? If you want to get your feet wet (so to speak), a small, natural pool is usually the easiest place to start.

ABOVE: Some gardens are filled with brilliant blooms to stimulate the senses. Others—like this Japanese garden—are green and peaceful. The designer made sure to include the traditional elements: water, an arching bridge, beautiful stones, and striking plant textures and forms.

RIGHT: What do you do with an old swimming pool that eats up half the garden? Here the landscape architect built a new concrete-lined, two-tier pond with a waterfall inside the old pool shell.

INSET RIGHT: Pools don't need to be big or fancy; for starters, you could simply sink a small rigid shell in the lawn. BELOW: This large natural pond shows the other end of the spectrum. It's nestled in a lush woodsy landscape, which reflects in the still water.

LEFT: The vivid purple bench overlooks a concrete pond with a fuchsia rim; the circular pond serves as a stage for aquatic plants growing in submerged pots. Hidden pipes carry water up through the columns, turning them into spill fountains.

BELOW: Birds and chipmunks feel right at home in this natural oasis amid dry California chaparral. To encourage their visits, a large portion of the garden area surrounding the pond was left unpaved. The colored concrete in the pond complements the golden, sandy soil. The low wall in back hides a fire buffer zone.

FACING PAGE: A formal terrace is lined with 24-inch bluestone tiles, which also line the nearby spa. In this case, the spa serves as a water garden, too.

THE RIGHT SITE

WHERE SHOULD YOUR NEW POOL GO? An obvious answer: Where you can enjoy it. Don't hesitate to look beyond the backyard. Consider a dramatic entry pond with an arched bridge; a quiet side-yard setting by the office window; a secluded corner tucked behind lush plants; or a courtyard koi pond. Tiny accent pools fit almost anywhere—or, if it's flowing water you're after, take a look at spill or wall fountains (see Chapter 2, "Fountains").

Put off by high bids, the home-owners decided to tackle this tiered concrete pond themselves. They had to hand-dig the soil, since there was no access for machinery, then make laminated forms to create the pond's curved edge. Stone coping and distinctive tiles complete the picture.

Before You Begin

First things first: Check any deed restrictions, setback requirements, and local ordinances that may affect the placement and design of your pool. In some areas, for example, standard-depth garden pools may be legally defined as "swimming pools" or some other type of "attractive nuisance." In that case, you might be required to install a fence around the pool or take other safety measures. Children are the biggest risk around a pool. If you have small children, consider a safer feature, such as a pebble-lined fountain or pondless waterfall with no standing water.

Check access to the site for supplies and any large equipment you might need. If plumbing and electrical hookups are required, make sure they're nearby.

Sun, Wind, and Weather

If you're planning to add plants or fish (see pages 22–23), consider the pool's location in relation to the sun. Most plants require at least 4 to 6 hours per day of sunlight. In the hottest climates, though, avoid the most intensely sunny locations; the water can get too hot, and it will evaporate very quickly. For fish,

you will need to provide a bit of shade or plan a deep pool that won't heat quickly.

The site should also be protected from wind and placed away from deciduous trees that will rain a steady supply of leaves and twigs into the water. Drainage is also important: Don't choose a low-lying or "bottom" area that will constantly overflow in wet weather.

When examining potential sites, remember that a sunny location in March may well be largely shaded by August. Could a simple screen or trellis help block seasonal sun?

An entire family pitched in to design and build this back-yard pond, with some help from their friends. They tore up the old brick paths and concrete slab with a jack-hammer. The new pond is bordered by flagstone and gravel, forming a natural counterpart to the faux-slate concrete beyond.

How do you build a water feature on sloping ground? One way is to go with the flow, linking a central pool with a series of descending falls or streams.

Coping with Slopes

Water seeks its own level, so it's easiest to build a pool on fairly flat ground. On the other hand, slopes are ideal spots for dramatic falls. You could terrace a slope by placing excavated dirt on the low side to create a berm, or by building one or more retaining walls. Once the pool area has been leveled, consider taking advantage of the slope by adding a waterfall or stream.

Before you begin digging, think about your view of the pool. If you install it up a hill, you may not be able to see the water from the patio or first-floor windows. On the other hand, that same spot might provide a great view from an upstairs bedroom.

Check It Out

Outlining your pool on the ground with rope, a garden hose, a trail of gypsum, or landscaper's spray paint will help you visualize it. Adjust the outline until the location is just right and the proportions are pleasing.

Plotting out related elements, such as a bog garden or a path leading to the water, will give you a sense of the overall effect. Lay a mirror on the ground to get a good idea of what the water will reflect. If you don't like what you see, reposition the pool or add a screen—perhaps a trellis or tall plants—to your plan.

When planning your pond, consider the view. In this case, warm wood decking seems to float on the water, providing the perfect platform for two casual chairs.

A 2¹/₂-foot-wide brick planter was converted into a raised pond by sealing the interior with concrete, then capping it with gran-ite blocks. A small pump provides aeration for water plants and a few goldfish—which in turn eat mosquito larvae.

PLANTS OR FISH?

IF PLANTS OR FISH WILL CALL YOUR GARDEN POOL HOME, FIRST TAKE TIME TO CONSIDER THEIR SPECIAL NEEDS. Fish and plants have different requirements for depth, surface area, and filtration. Chapters 4 and 5 provide detailed information on helping your pool's denizens thrive. But here are a few things to think about when you're starting out.

Planning a Water Garden

Water plants add color, shape, and texture to a pond, especially the hardy and tropical water lilies, oxygenating plants and grasses, and floating plants such as water hyacinths. A "bog" or border garden adjacent to the pool, receiving some overflow or splash, creates a special environment, perhaps with bright blue and yellow irises or papyrus catching the sun.

Because most plants require at least 4 to 6 hours per day of sunlight, a sunny site is the number-one prerequisite. You'll also probably want a ledge or shelf about 10 inches wide and 10 inches below the pool's edges, perfect for many submerged water plants. If you'll be raising fish, too, you may wish to build a divided pond or erect some other type of barrier: Fish think nothing of rooting your favorite water plants into oblivion.

Accommodating Fish

If you're considering the acquisition of a few gold-fish or koi, beware! You're almost certain to get hooked and want more.

Fish prefer a bit more shade than is optimal for plants, so site your pool accordingly. Pool depth is critical: A koi pond should be no shallower than 18 inches and ideally between 24 and 36 inches, or even deeper. It should have shallow places for feeding and fish-watching, and deeper water where the koi can go when surface water heats up or starts to freeze—or to escape a raccoon or the family cat. Don't use rough stone below the waterline, because fish can be injured by rubbing against the edges.

A koi pond will almost certainly require some form of pump for aeration and a filtering system for battling ammonia and other impurities in the water. For details, see pages 32–35.

FACING PAGE: Lush tropical plants and curved stone are hallmarks of a natural pool; here they're accented by swirling koi, which can be viewed from the small observation deck beyond.

A classic raised brick pool hosts an array of water plants and also makes a handy platform for displaying container plants.

ADDING EXTRAS

IS YOUR IDEAL POOL STARTING TO COME TOGETHER? Before you jump ahead, take time to consider the following amenities. Besides serving a practical purpose, each of these add-ons imparts design flair and helps give your pool a distinctive look.

• BORDERS AND EDGINGS can make or break your pool's appearance and the balance within the garden in general. The choice is broad: a grass lawn; an adjoining bog garden or rock garden; native stones and boulders; flagstones laid in a mortar bed; a wide concrete lip (especially useful as a mowing strip if grass adjoins the area); brick laid in sand or mortar; redwood or other rot-resistant wood laid in rounds or upright in columns; terra-cotta tiles; or railroad ties. For a closer look at edgings and installations, see pages 30–31.

• FOUNTAINS, WATERFALLS, AND STREAMS bring the sights, sounds, and refreshment of moving water to your landscape. To find the right fountain for your new pool, turn to Chapter 2, "Fountains." Want to make a broader statement? See Chapter 3, "Waterfalls and Streams."

• BRIDGES AND STEPPING STONES aren't just means to an end; they also add a classic touch to both formal and informal ponds and streams. For a look at their construction, see pages 100–101.

Pool lighting adds life at night. This entry pond features a combination of subtle light sources. Uplights accent water plants, while submerged pool lights create the water's glow and show off the waterfall.

Even the simplest bridge lets you admire your garden from a new perspective. Your span can be arched or flat; this gently arched bridge has curved sides cut from wider, straight boards.

• POOL AND PATH LIGHTS bring your garden alive at night. Is surface or submerged lighting best? Do you want low-voltage or line-voltage fixtures? Find answers on pages 38–39.

• OTHER HARDSCAPE FEATURES to keep in mind include pathways; privacy screens, arbors, and trellises; walls and fences; and built-in seats and benches. For complete details on these subjects, see the Sunset books *Trellises and Arbors*; *Fences, Walls & Gates*; and *Complete Patio*.

ABOVE: Ponds foster contemplation, so you might as well add a built-in bench. This one is formed from a level stone niche in the pond's retaining wall.
BELOW: Comfortably spaced stepping stones span a shallow pond.

NUTS AND BOLTS

ONCE UPON A TIME, PACKED CLAY AND STONE WERE THE ONLY CHOICES FOR A STURDY GARDEN POOL. THEN ALONG CAME CONCRETE. Some formal pools are still built with masonry materials—concrete, block, brick, tile, or stone—but today's do-it-yourselfer has two handy alternatives: flexible pool liners and rigid shells. Here's a closer look at your options.

Flexible Liners

These are the big news in garden pools, and you'll find some type of liner in nearly every home center and pond catalog. Installation is straightforward: Basically, you dig a hole, drape the liner over the inside, and fill with water. The typical charcoal color allows for maximum water reflection; you won't see the liner itself.

The least expensive choice among flexible liners is PVC plastic, which is most commonly available in a thickness of 20 millimeters. A carefully constructed pool lined with PVC can last up to 10 years, but PVC degrades under sunlight and develops leaks. It's also troublesome in cold climates. However, if you are on a budget and not particularly concerned about longevity, PVC may be a good choice.

Today's standard is EPDM. It costs more than PVC, but it's the better choice for a long-lasting, trouble-free pool. EPDM is a synthetic rubber material that stretches along with earth movements and climate variations. It holds up well to cold, heat, and intense sunlight. Pond-grade EPDM will not harm aquatic fish or plants. It's much thicker than PVC, typically 45 millimeters, and is sometimes guaranteed against defects for 20 years.

EPDM liner

Flexible liners come in rolls 5 feet wide or more, but most pool dealers will have about any width and length you need. How do you find the right size? Add twice the pool's depth to its width, then tack on an extra two feet; repeat this procedure to find the correct length. In other words:

Liner size = 2D + W + 2 ft. by 2D + L + 2 ft. So, for example, if your surface area measures 8 feet wide by 12 feet long and your pool is a maximum of 18 inches deep, buy a liner that is at least 13 by 17 feet.

If possible, wait until you dig the hole before ordering your liner, so you can be sure of the pool's final size. Ideally, the pool sides will slope in from the top at an angle of about 20 degrees. This prevents them from caving in and helps discourage pests.

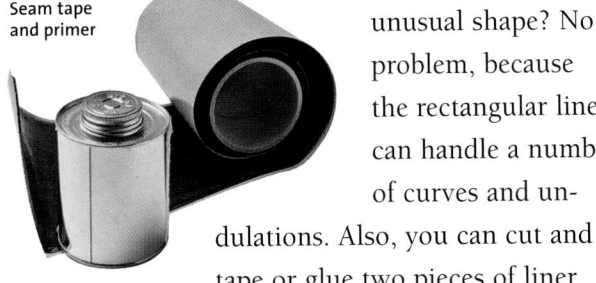

Seam tape and primer

What if you want an unusual shape? No problem, because the rectangular liner can handle a number of curves and un-dulations. Also, you can cut and tape or glue two pieces of liner together—ask your dealer to recommend the right seaming product for your type of liner.

Do you want shelves around the sides for plants? Normal pool-shelf dimensions are about 10 inches deep by 10 inches wide, but shelves of a variety of sizes, for boulders and other landscaping, lend the pool a more naturalistic look. You won't need to figure extra liner for shelves.

For a step-by-step look at installing a flexible liner, see pages 44–47.

Underlayment

Flexible liners should never be set directly on soil; instead, use some form of underlayment to protect the liner from being punctured by rocks or tree roots. Old carpet or a 1-inch layer of newspaper is often available at no cost and can work well. Sand, roofing felt, and carpet pad are other choices. You can also purchase underlayment material designed expressly for garden pools.

FLEXIBLE LINER OVERVIEW

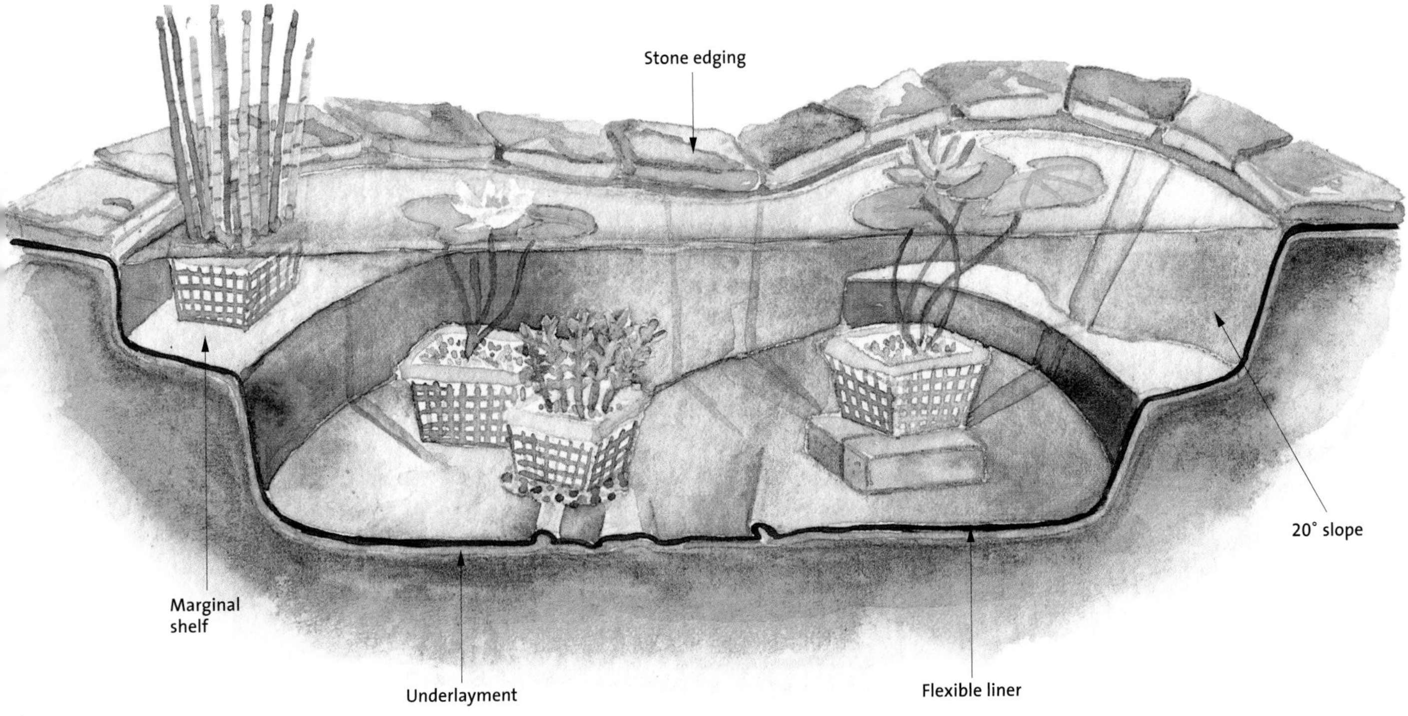

Stone edging

Marginal shelf

Underlayment

Flexible liner

20° slope

Rigid Shells

To picture these pool shells, think of a spa or hot tub buried in the ground and filled with plants and fish. Rigid shells are more expensive than flexible liners, but they come ready to go: Simply shape a hole that matches the shell's outline, add some sand, lower the unit into place, and backfill while adding water. For a walk-through, see pages 42–43.

Styles are limited: mostly circles, ovals, and kidney shapes. Sizes typically range from about 12 to 35 square feet of surface area. Most pools of this size are 18 inches deep. Some prefab modules can be joined to make larger units; others are available with waterfalls and small streams built in.

You can expect $\frac{1}{4}$-inch-thick fiberglass or polyethylene liners to last 20 years or more. These thicker products also work for raised pools (see page 49), since they require little extra support on the sides. Thinner plastic shells may last for only a decade, or even less if subjected to very cold temperatures.

Rigid shells are available at some garden centers and via mail-order catalogs and the Internet. Be sure to figure in shipping prices; transporting a large, noncollapsible shell can be expensive. When shopping in person, keep in mind that they are likely to appear larger in a garden store than they will in your yard.

Don't start digging until you have your shell. That way you can use the actual unit to mark the outline on your lawn, and you can test the depth of your hole with the shell itself instead of taking measurements again and again.

Plastic shell

RIGID SHELL OVERVIEW

Stone edging

Rigid shell

Level sand base

Concrete

Concrete still has its charms: It's the most plastic of materials, as well as the most adaptable. Its sometimes blank look can be disguised with stain or integral color, and it can be plastered for greater texture or water protection. Most concrete pools are reinforced with steel to withstand the pressure of soil and water.

Freeform concrete can be sloped up to 45 degrees with ordinary mix and can be pitched steeper with an air-sprayed, professionally applied mixture called gunite or shotcrete.

For crisp, perpendicular angles and walls, you'd need carpentered forms and poured concrete, which can be tricky and time-consuming to work with. For do-it-yourselfers, concrete blocks sometimes do the job better. Their greater size means quick assembly and fewer mortar joints per square foot of surface than other masonry units require, and they can be faced with tile, stucco, a stone design, or even brick.

You can also use block, brick, or stone to cap or cover a modern flexible liner—achieving, in effect, the best of both worlds.

Liner

CONCRETE BLOCK

Welded steel mesh

4"– 6" concrete

Spacer blocks

Gravel base

What about Wood?

Boats are made from wood, so why not pools? If you're handy with a hammer and the style suits your fancy, give lumber a look.

Support walls for raised and semiraised pools can be built either with standard 2 by 4 framing or with larger landscaping timbers laid in crisscross fashion. Both designs are shown on page 48.

The key to working with wood is not to labor over the interior details, but instead to line the inside with a flexible liner or rigid shell. A wide cap hides the liner edges and forms a perch for both plants and people.

ALL ABOUT EDGINGS

OFTEN, IT'S THE BORDER AROUND THE POOL THAT MAKES OR BREAKS YOUR POOL'S APPEARANCE AND balance within the garden in general. Edgings also serve several practical purposes. They protect the pool from damage, hide the liner material, and help keep debris from washing into the water. No matter what edging you select, the effect can be softened by adding plants around the perimeter.

When it comes to materials, the choice is broad: native rocks and boulders, bricks and flagstones laid in sand or mortar, a grass lawn, an adjoining bog garden or rock garden (often piled against a partially raised pool, or used at one end of a sloping site), a wide concrete lip (especially useful as a mowing strip if grass adjoins the area), redwood or other rot-resistant wood laid flat or upright in columns, terra-cotta tiles, and even railroad ties.

Pools don't need consistent edging around the entire perimeter. For example, the more accessible edges could be stone or brick, set on a firm foundation, while the remainder could be large boulders or grass.

Dry mortar mix

Bricks and stones

Large and small rocks are the most popular pool edgings. This edging looks even more natural if several of the largest rocks are partly submerged. In a

pond with a flexible liner, you'd do this by digging a shelf around the pool perimeter. Place the liner over this, set the rocks in place, and trim off any excess liner. If the ground is particularly soft around the pool, you may need to compact 3 or 4 inches of crushed rock around the edge to support the rocks and keep them from deforming the liner.

Boulders look best if partially buried; otherwise, prop them up with smaller rocks, then pack the area with soil and plantings. Here's one trick for placing large rocks: Break them with a sledge, move them piece by piece, and reassemble them with cement slurry. More back-saving tips: Slide a heavy rock on a large shovel, chain-link fencing, or board; or roll it, using a steel pipe or plank as a lever.

Crushed rock

Stone edging

Flexible liner

Flagstones and bricks lend a more formal look. For best results, set them on a 1-inch layer of sand or crushed stone that extends at least 2 feet out from the edge of the pool. Or the edges can be supported by a concrete foundation (shown at right) if they need to withstand heavy foot traffic. Gaps between stones or bricks can be filled with mortar, sand, soil, or fine gravel, or you can plant grass or other durable vegetation.

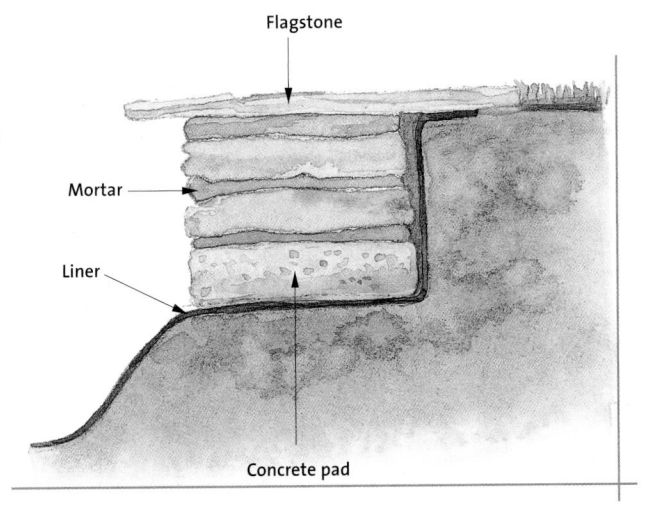

Flagstone

Mortar

Liner

Concrete pad

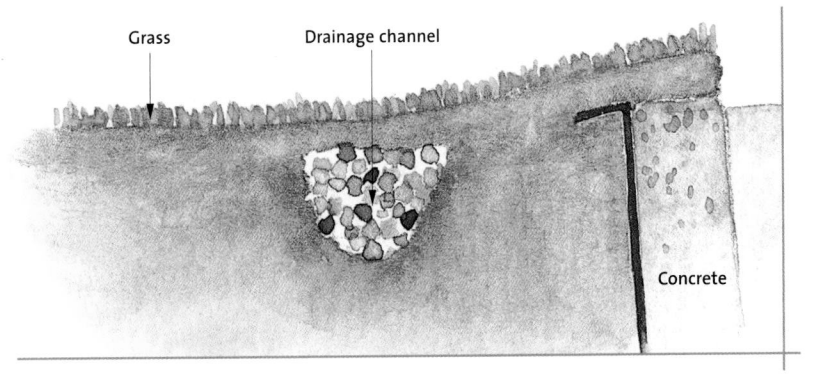

Grass

Drainage channel

Concrete

Grass is a terrific edging material if you want to soften the outline of your pool. But grass does present some problems. First, you need to keep grass clippings from blowing into the water when you mow. Second, if you expect the grass edges to be walked on regularly, you should build in support to prevent them from collapsing into the water. A concrete mowing strip, shown at left, helps solve this problem. You can then let the grass grow back over the concrete.

To prevent groundwater from spilling into the pool, build up the grass edge to slope away from the pool's sides, and consider digging a drainage channel around the pool. Fill the channel with gravel and direct it to a low point elsewhere in the yard.

A wood deck or walkway can run right up to and over the edge of a pool. Set the decking close to the water's surface or some distance above it, depending on your preference. In most cases, it's best to build the pool first, then construct a surrounding deck.

Other wood edgings include landscape timbers, sliced log rounds, and upright bamboo or log "rolls" (shown at right).

Log roll

POOL PLUMBING

SOME POOLS WON'T NEED ANY PLUMBING AT ALL, OR AT MOST A SMALL PUMP TO DRIVE A FILTER OR FOUNTAIN JET. Larger structures, such as fish ponds or those including a waterfall or stream, require more elaborate plumbing systems. Here's a rundown on choosing a pump and using filters, pipes, fittings, and other handy hardware.

Pumps

A pump serves three purposes: It helps aerate water, adding oxygen and promoting clean water for fish; it powers a pool filter; and it recirculates water to a fountain or waterfall. A pump also allows you to drain the pool in the event of a leak or for routine cleaning and maintenance.

Pumps come in two basic flavors: submersible and external. Submersible pumps are the most popular choice for garden pools. They sit on the bottom of the pool and are usually quiet and unobtrusive. They also tend to be less expensive than comparable external pumps. Good-quality submersible pumps have stainless-steel housings, use no oil, and are energy efficient. Attached strainers or screens block debris from clogging the pump.

Submersible pump

Large volumes of water and a constant demand—such as a biological filter system (see page 35)—favor an external pump housed outside the pool. Don't buy a pump designed for swimming pools; it's overly powerful and gobbles too much electricity. Instead, look for a pump that moves a higher volume of water at a lower pressure. Some models are self-priming, but many are not and need to be installed below water level to retain their prime.

What size do you need? Manufacturers give electrical specifications—amps, watts, and horsepower—for their products, and these are important because they measure how much electricity will be used to do the job. But the practical measure of a pump's performance is its head, the volume of water it will pump vertically. This tells you how many gallons per hour a pump can deliver at a given height.

Match your pump to the flow rate and lift required of it. A small fountain or waterfall and a filter might

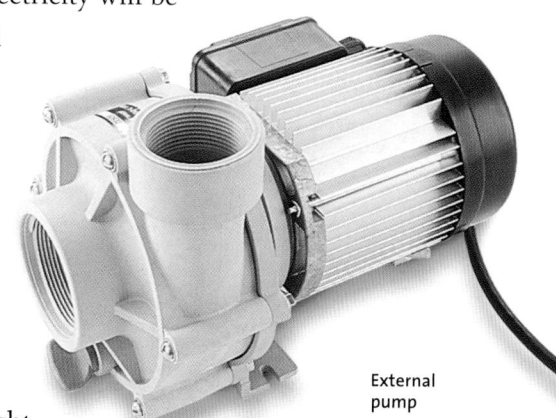

External pump

Calculating Pool Volume

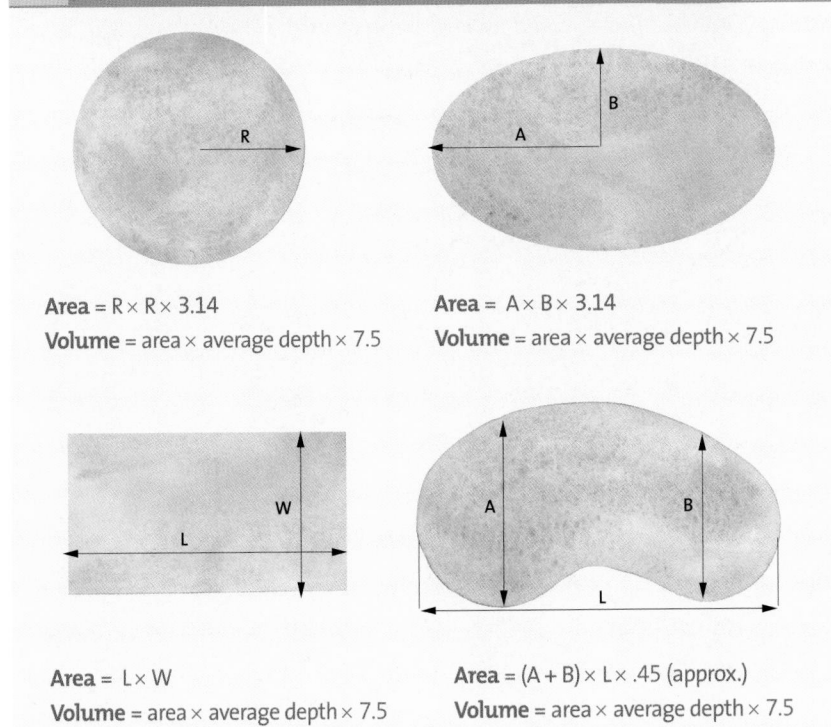

Area = R × R × 3.14
Volume = area × average depth × 7.5

Area = A × B × 3.14
Volume = area × average depth × 7.5

Area = L × W
Volume = area × average depth × 7.5

Area = (A + B) × L × .45 (approx.)
Volume = area × average depth × 7.5

Deciding on a pump, filter, water treatment, or fish medication all hinge on a working knowledge of your pool's capacity in gallons. Generally, to find a pool's volume, first calculate its area, which corresponds to the length times the width, then multiply the area by the average depth and a conversion factor of 7.5. The trick is finding the "length and width" of an informal pool! If you can't find a shape at left that approximates your pool, divide the outline up into units of simpler shapes, figure the volume of each chunk, and add them together for the total.

share a pump via a T-fitting or three-way valve (see page 37); a bigger load may call for two pumps.

In most cases, install the pump so that it has to move the water as short a distance as possible. For example, a waterfall pump is usually situated right at the base of the falls. The one exception is when the pump's primary function is to drive a filter. In this case, position the intake pipe—and the pump—at the opposite end of the pool to provide maximum circulation.

Elevate a submersible pump on bricks at the bottom of the pool to keep it free from silt and other pool debris. Alternatively, you may wish to form a small, gravel-lined pump vault at the bottom of the pool, covering the opening with removable wire mesh. If dirt and leaves will be problems, look for a solids-handling pump, as shown at right.

Solids-handling pump

Ideally, an external pump should be housed in a lidded vault to protect it and to eliminate clutter. You can camouflage the vault with rocks or plants or hide it behind a retaining wall.

Before placing your pump, consider how you'll supply it with electricity. For details, see page 38.

Filters

Filters help maintain a clean, healthy pool by trapping dirt, algae, and fish waste. To work properly, all the water in the pool should pass through the filter at least every two hours—or, in the case of fish ponds, every hour.

The three basic types of filtration are chemical, mechanical, and biological. An ultraviolet clarifier also helps keep pond water clear.

Chemical filtration simply uses algicides and other water-clearing agents to attack particular impurities. This is often the method of choice for a small tub or pool that has no plants or fish.

Mechanical filters use a straining mechanism to trap debris in the water. One type (shown below) circulates water through a box or cylinder containing pulverized fuel ash or activated carbon, zeolite, brushes, foam, or fiber padding. These devices are economical but tend to clog easily under heavy service (as in a fish pond), requiring frequent backwashing and/or replacement of the filter media. Most mechanical filters are powered with a submersible pump.

A beefier upgrade is the pressurized swimming pool filter. While they're quite efficient, these filters need a big pump to match, and they require regular back-flushing and a periodic change of sand.

Algicide

MECHANICAL FILTER

Gravel tray   Foam filter

Outlet

Plastic filter medium

Intake

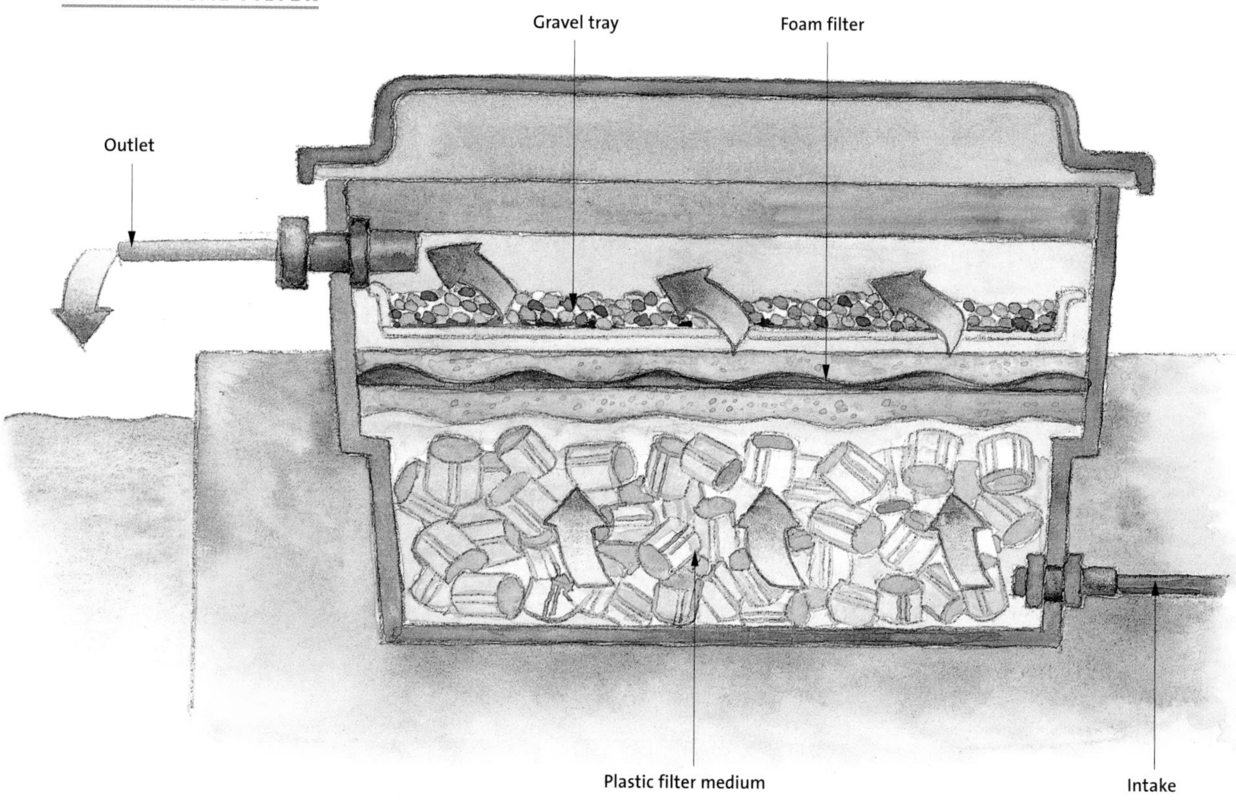

A biological filter is a variation on the mechanical theme, relying on pumped water to circulate up or down through a filtering medium. The difference is that the filter bed supports a colony of live bacteria that consume ammonia and harmful pathogens, converting them into nitrates for use by plants and fish. The system depends on the constant movement of water, and thus oxygen, through the filter to keep the bacteria alive. A reliable pump is a must.

The most popular and easy-to-use biological filters (such as the model shown at right) are installed outside the pool and can be disguised behind plants or rocks.

Biological filter

Ultraviolet clarifier

Ultraviolet clarifiers supplement your filtration system to make green pond water clear. These devices kill single-celled floating algae, but not the beneficial side- and bottom-growing algae. Both submersible and external units are available.

A pool skimmer works in tandem with the pump intake to pull dirt, pollen, floating algae, and leaves into the filtration system. The typical skimmer is made from heavy-duty ABS plastic and is housed in a hole dug at pool's edge (for details, see page 96). You can set a submersible pump right inside the skimmer. A skimmer is most effective when it's placed on the downwind side of the pool; the wind helps the pump by pushing debris toward the opening.

Skimmer

What about Mosquitoes?

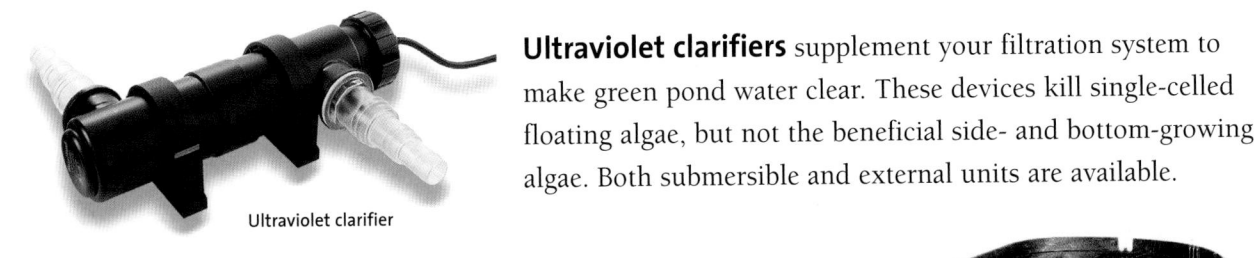

Mosquitoes aren't just a nuisance, they also pose a health risk. And, of course, they hatch in water. How do you keep your new pool or fountain from doubling as a breeding ground for swarms of biting insects? Since mosquito larvae need still, standing water to develop, aeration is one answer. A small fountain jet, spill spout, or waterfall can do the trick. So can a few goldfish, koi, or small mosquito fish (see page 129), which love to chow down on mosquito larvae. In fact, some county agencies will give you mosquito fish free. In a tub garden without fish, or in any water feature where the pump is off for long stretches, try mosquito rings (shown at left) or BT (see page 141). The floating rings last 30 to 60 days and target just mosquitoes—not plants, fish, or birds.

Mosquito rings

Clear vinyl

Black vinyl

Corrugated vinyl

Schedule 40 PVC

Schedule 80 PVC

Pipes, Fittings & Valves

Pipes and fittings allow water to flow in and around your garden pool. Valves let you control the rate and direction of that flow. Most of the plumbing supplies needed in a garden pool can be obtained from plumbing supply stores and home centers. When designing your pipe runs, remember that water flows best when it can flow straight, so try to minimize the number of sharp turns in the layout.

Pipes for indoor use are often made of metal, but plastic is the ticket for most pool projects. Plastic is inexpensive, easy to cut and assemble, and—unlike copper and other metals—it will not corrode outdoors.

Flexible pipe is the simplest to work with. Clear vinyl tubing is the least expensive, but black vinyl is stronger and withstands kinks and compressing. Corrugated vinyl costs more than other plastic pipe, but it can be bent around obstacles without kinking, which can cut the time and expense of having to install additional fittings. It can also be buried without collapsing.

If you need to use rigid pipe for an application, look for PVC, which is joined with solvent fittings. White Schedule 40 is the standard, but gray-colored Schedule 80 is stronger and blends in better.

For most garden pools, $1/2$-inch to $1 1/4$-inch pipe will suffice. To move large amounts of water, you may need to use $1 1/2$- or 2-inch pipe. Pipe sizes usually refer to the interior diameter (I.D.).

Coupling

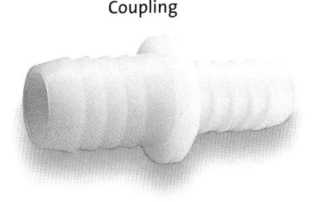

Stainless-steel clamps

Union

Tank adapter

Fittings join pipes to other pipes as well as to pumps and other equipment. Flexible plastic uses barbed (push-on) fittings and clamps for most connections, while PVC requires glue. Many types of fittings are available; some of the most common types for pools are shown above and at right.

T-fitting

Elbow fitting

Valves allow you to control the flow of water to a fountain or waterfall, divert water to a nearby drain, or shut down the entire system for repairs or maintenance. Well-placed valves can make your garden pool easier to use and more enjoyable.

A ball valve (shown at right) is handy for simple on/off use, and for isolating a pump, filter, or drain line. To control flow, opt for a gate valve. A three-way valve allows you to shut off the flow, send a controlled flow to a fountain head, or open up a line for draining the pool. Need to keep water flowing in one direction, or maintain a pump's prime? Install a check valve.

The float valve shown below automatically controls the level of water in your pool. Once attached to a water supply line and installed at the edge of the pool, the valve will top off water lost to evaporation and splash. Hide it under rock edgings or in an adjacent holding pool.

Ball valve

Gate valve

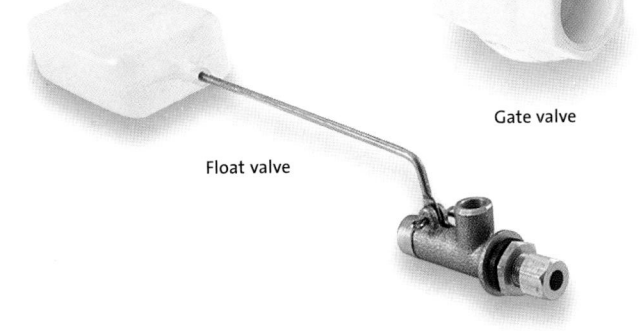

Three-way valve

Check valve

Float valve

GOING ELECTRIC

TO RUN A POOL PUMP, YOU'LL NEED A NEARBY 120-VOLT RECEPTACLE THAT'S PROTECTED BY A GROUND-FAULT CIRCUIT INTERRUPTER (GFCI), which immediately shuts off power to the line in the case of an electrical short or power leakage. In addition, all outdoor switches and outlets must have weatherproof covers.

GFCI receptacle

Well-placed lighting in or around your garden pool can bring your backyard alive at night. Lights also make it easier and safer to negotiate the area in twilight or darkness. When wiring your water garden, you have a choice of standard 120-volt or low-voltage fixtures.

Combination transformer/timer

Low-voltage systems, which use a transformer to reduce standard household current to 12 volts, are popular outdoors because they're safer, more energy efficient, and easier to install than standard 120-volt wiring. Low-voltage systems are great for lighting pathways, stairs, the edges of a pool, and even waterfalls. You can find a selection of fixtures and kits at electrical and garden pool supply stores as well as at home centers. Low-voltage lighting can be purchased in kit form or as individual components. For $50 to $100, you get a small transformer, about 100 feet of wire, and six to 12 lights of varying styles. However, by selecting the wiring, transformer, and fixtures individually, you get a much wider selection.

Installation is easy. With low-voltage wiring, there is little danger of people or animals suffering a harmful shock. The cable can lie on the ground, perhaps hidden by foliage, or in a narrow trench.

LOW-VOLTAGE SYSTEM

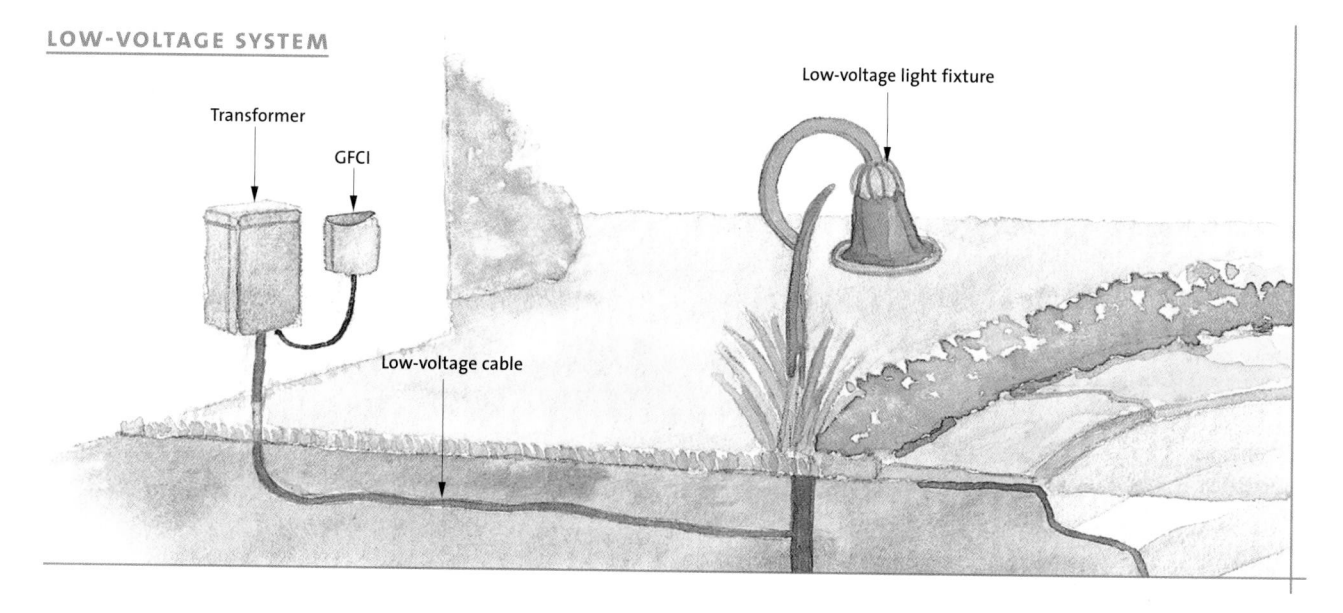

Transformer

GFCI

Low-voltage light fixture

Low-voltage cable

Get Control

How can you set up landscape lights or even fountains or waterfalls to take care of themselves? A timer is one solution. Two other options are daylight-sensitive photocells and motion-sensor fixtures or add-ons.

Outdoor timer

If your outdoor circuit begins indoors, you can control it with the same switches and timers you'd use inside the house. But if your system connects outdoors, choose a hardier outdoor timer, as shown at right.

Daylight sensors are simply photocells that react to daylight. When it's dark, the photocell sends power to the light fixture it's connected to. Come dawn, the sensor opens the circuit, shutting down the fixture.

Motion sensors can be purchased alone or integrated into a fixture that houses one or more floodlights. Some sensors have adjustable ranges and can be set to remain on for varying lengths of time.

A standard 120-volt system still has some advantages outdoors. The buried cable and metallic fixtures give the installation a look of permanence, and light can be projected a greater distance than is possible with low-voltage fixtures. If you want 120-volt lighting, it's best to plan for it before installing the pool. You may also need to secure an electrical permit. Code restrictions are particularly strict for installations in and near a pool.

Installing a 120-volt system is more complicated than installing a low-voltage one. Cable is usually run through conduit, which requires the use of special fittings and connectors. Unless you are quite comfortable with the materials and techniques, leave this work to an electrician.

Outdoor fixtures come in countless shapes and styles, but most fall into the following categories: general-purpose path lights; spotlights; broader floodlights; underwater lights; and those for pure decoration, such as rope lights, LEDs, and candle lanterns. Low-end fixtures are made of plastic, while high-end lights may be copper, bronze, or brass.

Outdoor fixtures

What's best, submerged or surface lighting? It's a matter of taste. Surface lighting can be adjusted with more subtlety and precision; also, fish and plants tend to look best when illuminated from above. On the other hand, underwater lights produce dramatic effects, which can be fine-tuned with a dimmer switch.

QUICK-AND-EASY IDEAS

WHEN IT COMES TO POOLS, BIGGER IS NOT ALWAYS BETTER. A small pool allows you to get your feet wet (so to speak) before tackling larger projects. It might be just the ticket for a compact garden, deck, or side yard sitting area—and if you don't like it, it's easy to move or take apart.

You could, of course, make a downsized version of any of the later projects in this chapter; but here are some initial quick-and-easy ideas. You might also want to take a look at Chapter Two, "Fountains," for other small but satisfying projects.

Bowls and Barrels

For those who aren't up for building an in-ground pool or who don't have room for one, containers provide an excellent way to enjoy a water feature without ever lifting a shovel.

Searching for the right container is half the fun. If you want plants (see page 117), buy at least a 25-gallon container, or build your own. Almost any leakproof vessel will do. A wooden half barrel is an attractive choice, and it's easy to find. For a more ornate pool, use a large decorative pot or urn.

If your container has a drain hole in the bottom, first plug it with a large cork, then seal the perimeter with waterproof silicone caulk.

Before placing a wooden, metal, or unglazed ceramic container in its permanent location, it's best to coat the inside with epoxy paint or line it with flexible PVC or EPDM. A dark-colored coating makes the water's surface more reflective.

Alternatively, you can place the main container inside a more handsome—but less seaworthy—barrel or tub. The tough plastic liner shown at right is sized to slip inside a half barrel. If you are so inclined, you could also bury the liner in the ground, then edge it with overhanging flagstones.

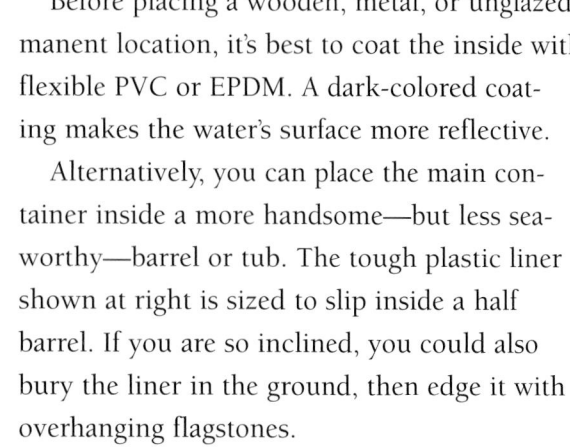

A rustic wood deck winds down past matching tub gardens, each formed from a half wine barrel.

RIGHT: This tough, water-tight liner slides right inside a half barrel.

A Concrete Waterhole

Assembling forms and reinforcement for a large concrete pool can be tricky—not to mention the prospect of pouring all that concrete! Here, a small free-form hole serves as the form. All you'll need are a shovel, a trowel, and a few sacks of ready-mix concrete, plus perhaps some dry cement color. It's easy—and if you don't like it, break it up and try again.

Aim for a concrete thickness of 2 inches or so. If you live in a cold climate, add several inches of gravel to the hole before you pour to help prevent frost heave. Let your water-hole cure for about a week, then brush on a coat or two of a clear concrete sealer and let dry before adding water.

Like a natural stone waterhole, this small concrete pool reflects the evening light and lush plants surrounding it.

1   **DIG THE FORM.** The hole you shape sets the tone for your water-hole. We dug a small, kidney-shaped hole with some cutouts for the edging rocks and boulders we planned to add later. The sides are gently tapered; the depth is about 12 inches, but it's not critical.

2   **MIX CONCRETE.** Empty ready-made concrete sacks into a wheel-barrow and sprinkle in some cement color as desired. Add water slowly, mixing the concrete thoroughly until it's plastic but not runny.

3   **SHAPE THE POOL.** Shovel the concrete into the hole and work it up against the edges. There's no science here; just form a pleasing bowl and round the top edges into an organic-looking shape. We used a rubber float to gently smooth the top surface as the mix was setting up.

You can leave things as is or, as we did, come back the next day to soften the look and make it more stonelike: Float some mortar on top, and sprinkle some cement color here and there. It's sort of like faux painting, in which you add extra layers and blend them with the layers below. We also spritzed the top coat with water so that it streaked and puddled, thus looking much like the staining inside a natural waterhole.

INSTANT POND

WHILE BUILDING A GARDEN POOL CAN BE TIME-CONSUMING, IT DOESN'T HAVE TO BE. The beautiful addition to the garden shown below can easily be built in a day or two, and the cost is quite reasonable. Much of the work is already done when you buy a rigid, preformed pool shell (see page 28). All you need to do is dig a hole large enough for the shell, edge it with your favorite stone, and choose the plants.

The owner of this pond installed a solar-powered pump and fountain, so he didn't need an electrical outlet. The fountain rests on the bottom of the pool; it's a good idea to anchor it with two or three flat rocks. If you choose a standard pump, you'll need a GFCI-protected electrical outlet nearby to power it.

Weathered flagstones hide the plastic lip of the shell. The stones look perfectly natural among the ornamental grasses and tufts of spreading, mossy-looking plants that grow around the pond.

A rigid shell was set in the ground, then ringed with weathered flagstones. Softly swaying ornamental grasses make a dramatic backdrop for this small pond; pink-flowered thrift and sedum grow up front.

1 **MARK THE OUTLINE.** First, choose a flat, open area with plenty of sunshine. Remove sod and any plants. Set the pool shell, right side up, in place and scratch its outline in the soil with a stick. Then remove the shell and make a more visible outline with sand or flour.

2 **DIG THE HOLE.** Next, excavate a hole 2 inches deeper and 2 inches wider than the shell, to accommodate a cushioning layer of sand. Remove any roots and rocks as you work. Use a carpenter's level to make sure the bottom of the hole is flat. As you work, test the fit with the shell itself. When the hole is ready, pour 2 inches of sand into the bottom and set the shell inside.

3 **FILL AND BACKFILL.** Make sure the shell is level and flush with the surrounding surface; remove the shell as needed to make any adjustments. Start filling the shell with a slow trickle of water. At the same time, begin backfilling by adding about 4 inches of sand around the outside of the shell. Tamp the sand down, then add another layer. When the filling and backfilling are done, pack some extra soil under the shell's lip to help support it.

4 **ADD THE EDGING AND THE FOUNTAIN.** Edge the pond with stones to hide the shell's rim. Make sure that most of each stone's weight rests on soil, not on the shell. Set the fountain in the pool, anchor it with stones, and plug it in. Adjust its position to suit your taste. Cover the power cord with mulch or run it through a shallow trench, then add the plants of your choice.

A NATURAL POOL

THE OWNER OF A THOUGHTFULLY DESIGNED GARDEN WAS VERY HAPPY WITH HER CREATION. But she felt it lacked one important element—the sight and sound of

ABOVE: A flexible liner allows you to make a pond nearly any size, shape, or style you want. This pool appears to have been formed by nature, with curves that mimic those found in the wild. Stone edgings and a small waterfall complete the picture.

water. After considering several options, she decided to carve out enough room for a small garden pool (shown above) equipped with a modest waterfall and an adjacent bog garden, which would allow for greater plant diversity. The space limitation, coupled with the desire for a free-form, natural-looking water feature, made the choice of a flexible EPDM liner (see page 26) an easy one.

Perhaps the biggest hurdle was getting electrical power to the desired location for a pump outlet, which was behind the proposed waterfall (see page 47). This entailed removing a number of patio pavers, digging a trench, and running electrical cable through buried PVC conduit to a GFCI outlet.

The homeowner ordered the liner and underlayment from a local garden-pool supplier. The pebbles, flagstone, and mulch came from a well-stocked landscaping supplier. A nearby home center was the best choice for the pump, vinyl tubing, tools, electrical supplies, and last-minute materials.

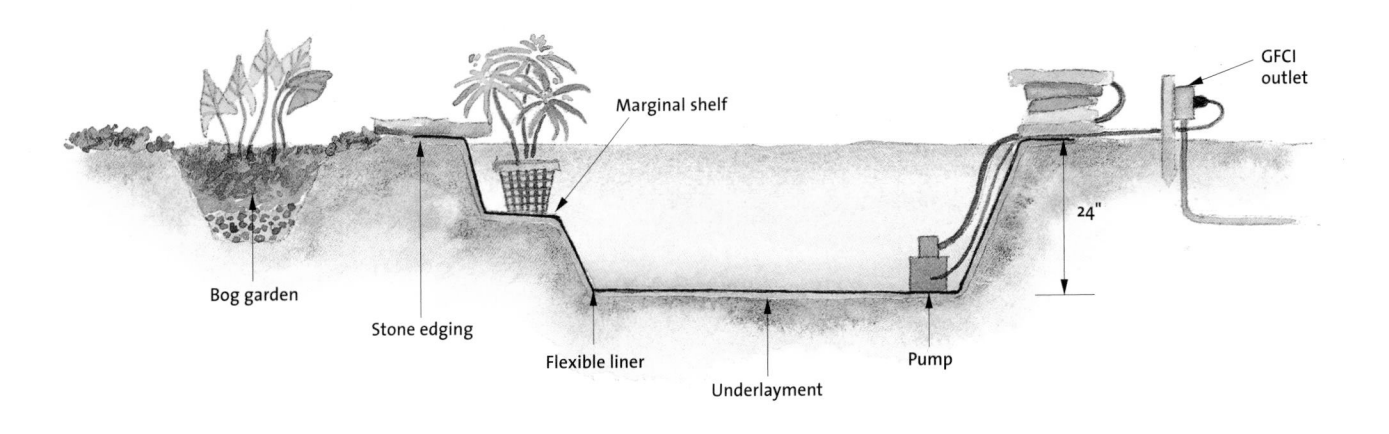

GFCI outlet

Marginal shelf

24"

Bog garden

Stone edging

Flexible liner

Underlayment

Pump

1 **DIG THE HOLE.** First, lay out several pool shapes with a garden hose until you find one you like. A curving, irregular pond looks most natural; try to avoid sharp bends or corners, which are difficult to line. When you're satisfied, mark the final outline with landscaper's spray paint or sand. Start excavating with a sharp shovel or spade. As you dig, snip off stray roots and remove stones. If you find a significant number of roots, reshape or shift the pool outline to avoid damaging a desirable plant. Dig the entire pool down to the height of the marginal shelves (see illustration above). Mark the edges of the shelves as you did the perimeter, then dig out the rest of the pond. It's best to put off purchasing the liner until after the hole is dug, so you can calculate the exact size that you need.

2 **CHECK LEVEL.** Set a long 2 by 4 across the hole and use a carpenter's level to check that the sides are of equal height. If they're uneven, use some of the excavated soil to build a berm around the low side. Leave the 2 by 4 in place and use it as a guide to measure the depth of the hole and of the marginal shelves, digging and filling as needed.

continued ▶▶

3 **ADD UNDERLAYMENT.** A first layer of underlayment protects the pool liner from being damaged by sharp rocks or roots. Use stones to hold the underlayment in place until the liner is added. An alternative to using underlayment is to install 2 inches of sand on the bottom and sides of the hole. However, if you take this route, be sure to make the hole deeper to accommodate the sand.

4 **INSTALL THE LINER.** Drape the liner to follow the contours of the hole as closely as possible. EPDM liner will stretch as it's filled with water, but it's best to minimize this. Use heavy stones or concrete blocks to hold the edges of the liner in place before you add water. If you wish, you can also cover the bottom or the marginal shelves (or both) with smooth pebbles or river rocks to conceal and protect the liner.

5 **FILL THE POOL.** Begin slowly filling the pool with a garden hose. At the same time, start smoothing the liner into shape. Some creases are inevitable, but they can be minimized by careful fitting and adjusting. Particularly unsightly wrinkles can be covered with rocks or plants. One brave soul will probably need to wade into the pool to do this.

6 **LAY THE EDGING.** With the pool nearly filled, begin installing the edging. Using a utility knife, trim several feet of the liner at a time; add edging stones; then trim more liner. Pack a little extra soil here and there to level the top layer of stones.

Want a Waterfall?

A simple waterfall can be built with stacked rocks that conceal a water supply tube rising from a submersible pump placed in the pool. Run the tubing up behind the first course of rocks, leaving plenty of extra length for adjustments. Once the rocks are arranged to your liking, add mortar or pure silicone caulk between layers. Two waterfalls can flow simultaneously from each side of the rocks, as shown at left. A few well-placed plants will hide the plumbing. For more waterfall ideas, see Chapter Three, "Waterfalls and Streams."

ABOVEGROUND OPTIONS

RAISED POOLS CAN BE ACCESSORIZED JUST LIKE IN-GROUND VERSIONS, BUT they provide a different type of presence in the landscape. They are easy to approach, and when surrounded by sturdy walls and a wide cap, they invite visitors to sit and enjoy the pool. Raised pools are also a bit safer, as one is less likely to step into the water accidentally, and many people find them easier to access for cleaning and maintenance.

Here are two possibilities: a rustic stacked-timber pool and a raised-shell pool. Alternatively, of course, you can build your raised pool from concrete blocks, as shown on page 29.

OPPOSITE: When your ground is hard and rocky, a raised pond is a good option. The base of this shell was set just a few inches into the ground. Dry-stacked stones hide the sides of the shell and provide planting pockets.

Stacked-Timber Pool

Support walls for raised pools can be built with landscaping timbers, railroad ties, or wood-stud framing, as an alternative to stone walls. The key is to line the inside with a flexible liner or rigid shell so the wood needn't be waterproof. The pool can be completely aboveground; or, for a lower profile (and to save on lumber), you can first dig a hole to partially recess the pool, line it with underlayment or sand, and then place the liner or shell.

Cap

Liner

Landscape timbers

These weathered timbers were stacked in crisscross shape, then capped with 1-by lumber, forming a sturdy, rustic raised pond.

In the photo below left, metal strap ties reinforce the corners of the walls. Another option is to drill matching vertical holes in each layer of wood, then drive galvanized pipe or threaded rod down through the holes into the ground, staking them in place. A decorative cap trims the top and serves as a garden seat or plant shelf.

Or build a wood frame that's just like house walls, as shown at right. The inside is lined with EPDM or a rigid shell. Cover the outside with horizontal siding, cedar shingles, tile, or whatever else you wish.

Wood siding

Liner

Cap

Pressure-treated 2 x 4 framing

Raised English Pool

For this project, the shell's plant shelves rest at ground level, with just the lowest base section underground. A stone wall that matches the existing walkway hides the aboveground portion of the shell. The dry-stacked wall also has the advantage of allowing the homeowner to place pockets of soil between the stones, so that plants can grow from the crevices.

Prepare the site and install the shell as outlined on pages 42–43—only here, there's much less digging!

Then surround the exposed upper portion of the shell with dry-stacked stones—flat flagstones work best. Place the first layer a few inches away from the shell and check to make sure that it is fairly level. Fill in the gaps between shell and stones with soil. Then stack each succeeding layer closer to the liner, backfilling with soil to help support both the shell and the wall. Slowly fill the pond as you go.

Build up the stone layers until the surround is even with the top edge of the shell. Then mortar a final course of stone to the top layer, using the longest flat rocks you have. Allow them to hang over the lip of the liner by about 2 inches to hide the shell's rim and add a sense of depth.

Leave a small space between stones and shell, then backfill with topsoil while slowly filling the shell with water.

fountains

WHETHER IT SPILLS, SPLASHES, OR SPRAYS, A FOUNTAIN MASKS NEIGHBORING NOISE AND ADDS COOLING MOISTURE TO THE AIR. SMALL FOUNTAINS MAKE GREAT DO-IT-YOURSELF PROJECTS AND FIT ALMOST ANYWHERE— EVEN INDOORS. LARGE WALL FOUNTAINS ARE ELEGANT ADDITIONS TO PRIVATE PATIOS OR COURTYARDS.

SPILL FOUNTAINS

SOME FOUNTAINS SPILL, OTHERS SPRAY OR SPLASH. In spill fountains, the water simply follows gravity. Because there's little overspray, these fountains can often fit into small spaces—even indoors.

A spill fountain requires no more than a spout and a watertight container of your choice. A small submersible pump sits on the bottom of the container and sends water via tubing to the spout, where it spills out. Some versions dispense with the spout and let the water overflow from one container into a larger watertight basin below. For a closer look at this setup, see page 66.

Although spouts and basins make classic spill fountains, consider other interesting options, such as those shown here. Or invent your own. Whatever you use for the fountain, you'll need a hole in its bottom for the supply tubing. Drill one if necessary.

A more formal effect is provided by a fountain statue, such as the one shown on page 66. Fountain statues come self-contained or can be set in a pool on a hollow pedestal. They can also be placed around pool edges so that the water spills back into the pool.

Or let water spill from one shelf or vessel to another, like a tiny waterfall. Spill pans are available in two- and three-tiered plastic or metal sets at garden supply stores and through the Internet. You can also make a series of spill pans or containers from your own materials. Need ideas? Just turn the page.

FACING PAGE: A bamboo spout splashes water into a carved, polished-rock basin—which in turn feeds a tiny pool, where it's recirculated. Red azaleas ring the spot.

This tabletop fountain of stacked, geometric stones is like a portable spring, bringing the sound of trickling water just about anywhere.

A glazed blue oil-jar fountain sits on a tile-covered pedestal. A submersible pump housed within the pedestal pushes water through a galvanized pipe, which fits through a hole in the jar's bottom. The water then spills over the jar's rim and into the square, concrete-lined pool.

A water bowl of Mexican canterra stone burbles in a casual, gravel-lined courtyard. The 42-inch-wide bowl sits on an industrial-strength grate atop a wide concrete basin.

Looking for a novel fountain spout? This large gunnera leaf continually drips water into a small, stone-capped pool.

These "rain chains" of hand-hammered copper cups direct water down to a matching basin. They're designed as gutter downspouts, but try them anywhere you can feed them water.

ABOVE: Copper spill pans cap a descending string of concrete drain pipes, forming a freestanding cascade. BELOW: Almost any spout and basin can make a spill fountain—for instance, this clay teapot and matching teacup.

SPRAY AND SPLASH FOUNTAINS

SPRAY FOUNTAINS HAVE HEADS THAT SHOOT WATER UPWARD IN PATTERNS RANGING FROM MASSIVE COLUMNS TO SPRAYS AS DELICATE AS LACE. Popular spray heads include bell, mushroom, and calyx domes; cascade, swivel, and aerating jets; multitiered patterns; and spray rings with multiple, adjustable jets. Frothy heads sit above the water, while bubblers well up from just below the surface. Splash sculptures add spray jets to statues or other figures.

Contrary to their appearance, most spray fountains are not water guzzlers; in fact, few are hooked up to water supply lines at all. A submersible or recirculating pump recycles the pool water and feeds it back to the spray jet, where it's used again and again. The jet is threaded to a riser pipe or tubing, which in turn is fixed to the pump. For details, see page 66.

The main design rule for spray fountains is this: Use a short, heavy column of water in windy spots. Go for height, distance, or drama only where the spray will not scatter widely.

Try to place a spray fountain against a background that highlights the water's movement. Water in a heavy column tends to be translucent, so backgrounds should be darker. Fine sprays look best when outlined against a plain, flat surface.

In general, the pool diameter should be at least twice the spray's height. The fountain jet is usually installed just above the water level.

If your pool will include water plants or fish, plan the installation carefully. Many water plants, especially water lilies, do not like heavy turbulence. Fish tend to avoid the area near a fountain, though the aeration provided by the moving water is good for them.

FACING PAGE: A classic splash fountain holds center stage in this Tuscan-inspired courtyard.

A sculptural granite sphere was drilled for a bubbling riser pipe; the bronzed bird atop the pedestal gets a perpetual cool drink.

A bubbler fountain sits inside a colorful tiled pool, providing plenty of splash and enough water for thirsty bees, too.

Want a novel spray fountain? Improvise! Here, an old claw-foot tub forms the basin, which overflows from the exuberant fountain head in its center. The water continues down a rock-lined stream.

A large urn, which looks right at home in this collection of "found objects," houses a fountain head just below the water surface. Glass pebbles and gravel hide the basin below.

The spray's source is underground and, except for a small opening for the fountain head, completely covered with tightly fitted, vertically stacked flagstones.

WALL FOUNTAINS

WALL FOUNTAINS WERE PRACTICAL PUBLIC WATER SOURCES LONG BEFORE THE INVENTION OF INDOOR PLUMBING. Today, of course, their main role is ornamental, bringing the sight and sound of running water to the garden.

FACING PAGE: This wall fountain is right at home in a clean, contemporary setting; the colored-concrete spill shelf is joined by vibrant plaster walls and a limestone-lined holding pool.

Water spouts from the mouth of a cast-stone ram's head onto a shell-like shelf, then spills into the crescent-shaped basin, where it's pumped back up to the top.

Although it may look different, a wall fountain operates like most other fountains: Water recirculates from a basin or pool through plastic tubing or pipes to the outlet. Water can pour directly into the pool from the pipe, overflow from a basin, or spill from a series of shelves or trays. An increasingly popular variation adds a whimsical touch to today's swimming pools and spas. Water issues from lions' and gargoyles' mouths, wall niches, spill shelves, or gleaming, high-tech nozzles into spa or pool—sometimes via a chain of streams or waterfall-joined holding pools.

Fountain masks—such as those lion or gargoyle faces—are readily available and are frequently installed on existing walls, but you can hang one just about anywhere you like. The trick is to hide the outlet pipe and support. Although the traditional lion's head spewing water springs to mind, almost any item can be used to create this feature. It might be a sheet of clear or stained glass with water running down its face; a gnarled driftwood branch with small containers mounted on it so that water runs from one to the next; or an old metal watering can with water pouring from its spout.

Whatever you choose to hang on the wall, the components are always the same: a basin containing a submersible pump, tubing from the pump to the fountain spout, and water falling back to the basin. For a closer look at what's involved, see pages 66–67.

Designing a classic wall fountain from scratch is a bigger job. Not only are the wall and holding pool tricky to build, but the surrounding area must have complementary features if the fountain is to fit into its environment. The good news? It's much simpler to plumb the wall and pool as they're being built.

LEFT: This modern take on the wall-fountain theme includes a simple pipe spout spilling into a basin lined by colorful cubes. The right-angled pipe appears to come from the wood fence. BELOW: A classic tile fountain adds ambience to an enclosed front courtyard.

Fountains can be art, too. Here, water spills from a shiny chrome elbow, then ping-pongs down a glass stairway. It's all set off by a screaming purple wall.

Water doesn't only spill from lions' heads or milkmaids' jars; here, it issues from the mouth of man's best friend.

Nuts and Bolts

READY TO ADD A FOUNTAIN TO YOUR LIFE? YOU CAN PURCHASE ONE READY-MADE, ASSEMBLE your own from individual parts, or even go all-out and build a wall fountain from scratch. The key to most fountains is a small submersible pump—see page 32 for details. Here's a closer look at the other hardware you'll need.

Fountains to Go

The simplest and least expensive way to add a fountain is to buy a small, complete unit from a garden center, pool catalog, or Web site. No plumbing is required. You simply put the kit together, fill the bowl with water, add an algicide, and plug it in to a nearby GFCI outlet.

Garden centers and statuary stores also stock freestanding ceramic fountains and sculptures. Freestanding fountains have a water reservoir containing a small submersible pump that powers the fountain. Spray fountain assemblies include a pump, strainer, valve, and fountain head (and in some cases, lights), all mounted in a single, compact, submersible base; you pick the pool.

Splash sculptures and statues can also be set inside a pool. If the combined weight of the statue and pedestal exceeds 100 pounds, a concrete footing should be placed under the pool liner, as shown on page 66. Sometimes it's simplest to set these fountains on dry land and let them spill or splash back into the pool.

Ready-made wall fountain

Freestanding fountain

Build Your Own

Once you have the basics down, it's relatively easy to design and build your own spill fountain. For a look at how they work, see the drawing on page 66. Then turn to pages 68–71 in the project section. Maybe one of those designs is just right; if not, it might be adaptable to what you have on hand.

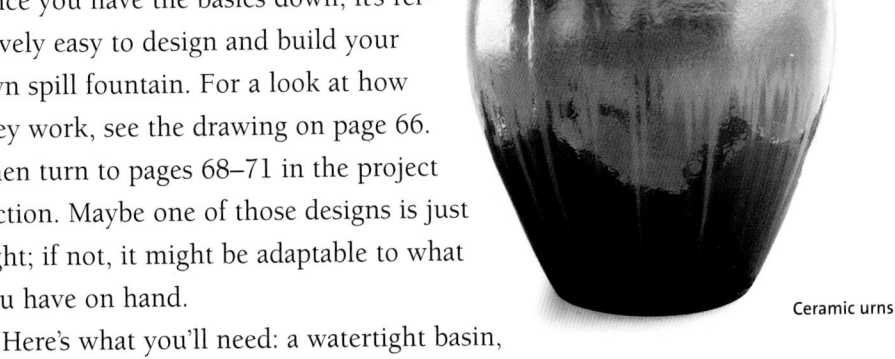
Ceramic urns

Here's what you'll need: a watertight basin, a submersible pump, some vinyl tubing, and, in some cases, a separate spout. A small pump and spout are shown below right. A gate valve or three-way valve (page 37) allows you to fine-tune fountain output to anything from a soothing trickle to a hearty roar.

A sampling of spray jets and heads is shown below right. Though some spray fountains come as complete kits, others include the jet or head only, requiring a riser pipe to achieve the proper height. Choose threaded Schedule 80 PVC for best results. These gray-colored pipes, commonly used for sprinkler heads, are sold as "nipples" in several lengths and diameters. Fasten the riser tightly to a stake or support block, if necessary, and connect it to the pump's outlet opening. Then screw the jet onto the riser's threads. Most spray fountains can be powered by a submersible pump, but large volumes of water may call for large pipes and an external pump (see page 32).

Bamboo spout and pump

Whether your fountain sprays or spills, you'll also need a 120-volt, GFCI-protected receptacle for the pump, a switch and perhaps a timer to control the fountain, and a separate switch for any optional fountain lighting.

Spray jets

Submerged, movable light fixtures (page 39) positioned directly below the spray create the most drama; low-voltage halogen downlights are effective for pinpointing special features. Timers and color blenders that are programmed to automatic sequences can also be purchased for submerged light fixtures.

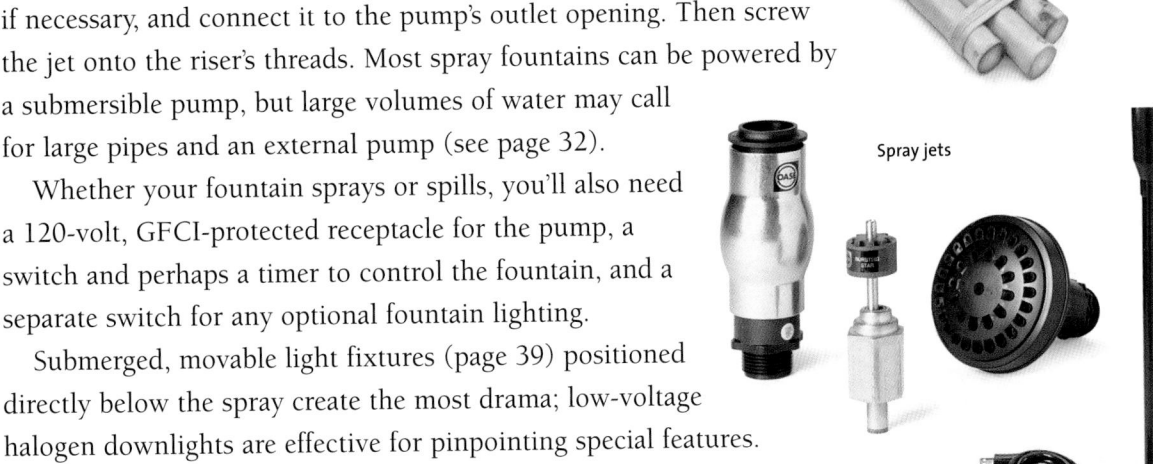
Spray fountain kit

A SPRAY FOUNTAIN

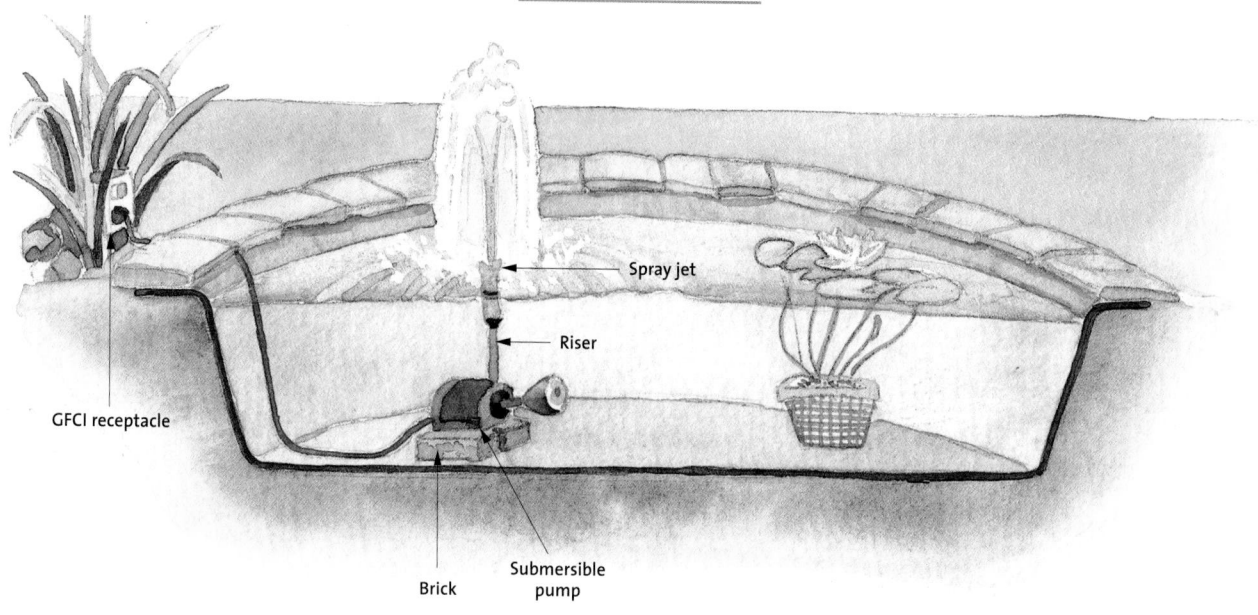

Spray jet

Riser

GFCI receptacle

Brick

Submersible pump

A SPLASH SCULPTURE

Tubing

Brick pedestal

Submersible pump

Concrete footing

A SPILL FOUNTAIN

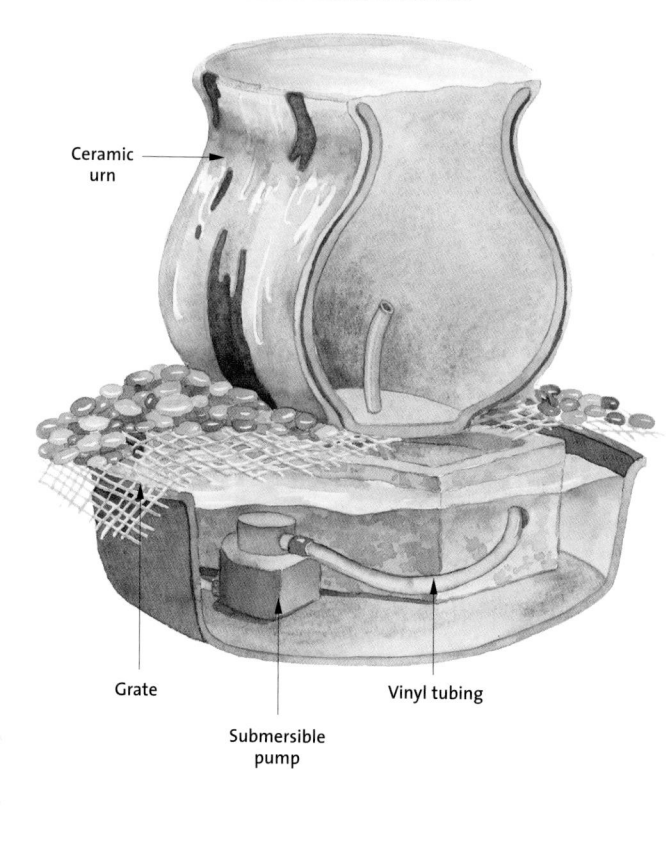

Ceramic urn

Grate

Vinyl tubing

Submersible pump

What about Wall Fountains?

Building a classic wall fountain from scratch is relatively expensive. For a look at what's involved, see the drawing below right. You'll need a wall, of course—plus a pump, some pipe or tubing, and a water-tight basin or holding pool.

Cover the pipe end with a decorative noz-zle or figurine, or hide it between masonry units, leaving a narrow slot in mortar or grout. An electrical switch, per-haps located indoors, controls the pump-driven flow; a gate or three-way valve allows you to adjust the flow to match the mood. If you wish to automatically top up water lost to evaporation, hook up a float valve (page 37) to your water supply line.

The construction of the raised holding pool is critical: Concrete or concrete block work well, covered with plaster or faced with brick, tile, or stone above the water level. To leak-proof any holding pool, you can line the inside with a flexible liner (see page 26).

Sound hard? There is an easier, though less formal-looking, route: Buy a ready-made fountain mask, like the one shown on pages 74–75. Simply hang the mask on an existing wall and add the pump, pipe, and holding basin of your choice.

The trick, though, is routing the pipe. Construction is much simpler if plumbing is incorporated into the wall during the building process. Ideally, you'd drill holes in an existing wall to route the pipe behind it from basin to mask. In real life, some improvising may be required: Clear tubing blends in best, and you can further hide it with vines, lattice, or a trellis set off from the wall.

Spill pan

Holding basin

A WALL FOUNTAIN

Fountain mask

Vinyl tubing

Brick

Submersible pump

Holding basin

CONTAINER FOUNTAIN

YOU DON'T NEED A BACKYARD TO HAVE A WATER FEATURE. A small one like the container fountain shown below can be added to any space, indoors or out, where you want the tranquil sound of trickling water. All you'll need is a container, a pump small enough to fit into that container, a spout, a little tubing, and some other amenities of your choice.

This project features a variation on a traditional Japanese design called the *shishi-odoshi,* or "deer scarer." Since bamboo is mostly hollow, you can easily make a bamboo pipe and spout yourself, though you may need to do some drilling to completely hollow out the stalk. Tie the pieces together using decorative twine or copper wire, which will eventually turn a pleasant green. Or buy a preassembled bamboo fountain from a nursery or pool-supply source.

POTPOURRI

The pot used in this project was sealed and glazed. If the one you choose is not watertight, you can apply a coat of acrylic masonry sealer or epoxy paint. If your container has a hole in the bottom, plug it, and then cover the plug with a layer of pure silicone caulk. Once dry, the caulk will provide a firm seal.

A classic bamboo spout pours water into a glazed basin dressed with small stones and plants. A tiny hidden pump provides the flow.

1 **SET UP THE PUMP.** First, rinse out the container and wash the rocks. Then attach a piece of clear vinyl tubing to the pump's outlet. Place the pump on the bottom of the container, with a few rocks around it to hold it in place.

2 **ADD A PLANT AND ROCKS.** Choose a plant that grows in water, like this miniature umbrella plant, and place it in a submersible dish. The bonsai dish was chosen to add color because it will be seen, but any kind will do. Place the plant dish on the bottom of the container and snake the pump's power cord behind it. Add more rocks to hold everything in place.

3 **INSTALL THE FOUNTAIN.** Thread the tubing up through the bamboo and place the bamboo on the edge of the container. Then pull the rest of the tubing through, cut off any excess, and attach the spout. Aim the spout toward the spot you want to hit with water.

4 **ADD WATER AND TEST.** Arrange some flat pieces of slate or flagstone. Fill the container with water—the water level needs to be only slightly higher than the pump. Plug in the pump and check that the water moves smoothly through the tubing. Whenever the pump makes a humming sound, more water is needed.

A SPILL FOUNTAIN

THE QUIET SPLASHING OF AN URN FOUNTAIN CAN SUBTLY CHANGE THE MOOD OF THE GARDEN—and of the gardener. The fountain shown below left is large enough to be a presence in the yard, yet small enough to be assembled in a few hours. The magical effect is created by hiding a plastic basin underground to catch the falling water; a small pump in the basin sends water back to the pot.

When deciding where to put your fountain, consider a spot where colorful foliage or unobstructed blue sky will reflect in the water. Choose a pot with a slight texture and a color or glaze that looks good when wet, to emphasize the sheeting effect. The pot can be short and stout, tall and curvy, or anything in between.

The pot will need a hole drilled in the bottom. If yours doesn't have a hole already, drill one with a suitable bit. To catch the falling water, the diameter of the plastic basin that sits below the pot should be at least 3 inches wider than the diameter of the pot itself. The depth of the basin need not be more than a few inches higher than the pump.

This elegant ceramic urn is plumbed to spill water over the sides and into a plastic basin, where a submersible pump sends the water back to the pot.

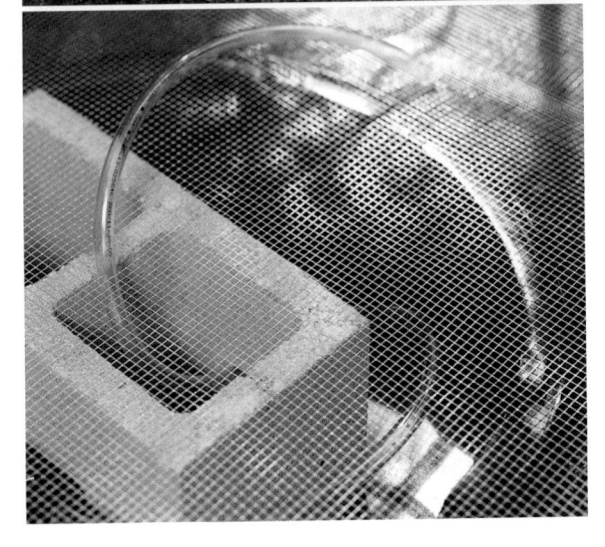

1. **INSTALL THE BASIN.** Dig a hole as deep as the plastic basin, and 2 inches wider. Center the basin in the hole and check that the rim is level. To support the sides, backfill the hole with some of the excavated soil. Tamp down the soil and check again to see that the basin is level; adjust as necessary.

2. **ADD A CONCRETE BLOCK.** With a masonry bit, drill a hole for the vinyl tubing in one side of a concrete block. Place the block in the basin (the block will support the weight of the pot). Place the submersible pump in the basin. Slide one end of the vinyl tubing over the pump's outlet. Snake the other end through the hole in the block toward the center of the basin; you'll be coming back to it later. Meanwhile, lead the pump cord out of the tub and toward a GFCI outlet.

3. **INSTALL WIRE MESH.** Cut a piece of heavy-gauge wire mesh at least 6 inches wider than the basin, and lay it over the top. Using tin snips, cut a hole in the center of the mesh, making it wide enough for the vinyl tubing to pass through easily. Bend the cut edges of the mesh back so that they won't poke the tubing.

4. **POSITION THE POT.** Lower the pot onto the mesh, centering it on the concrete block. As you lower, pull the tubing through the pot's drainage hole; it should reach halfway up the interior of the pot. Make sure the pot is level. Spread silicone caulk around the drainage hole and tubing and let it cure. Spread pebbles over the wire mesh, placing most of the larger pebbles toward the edges. Trim off any excess mesh. Finally, fill both the pot and the basin below it with water and plug in the pump.

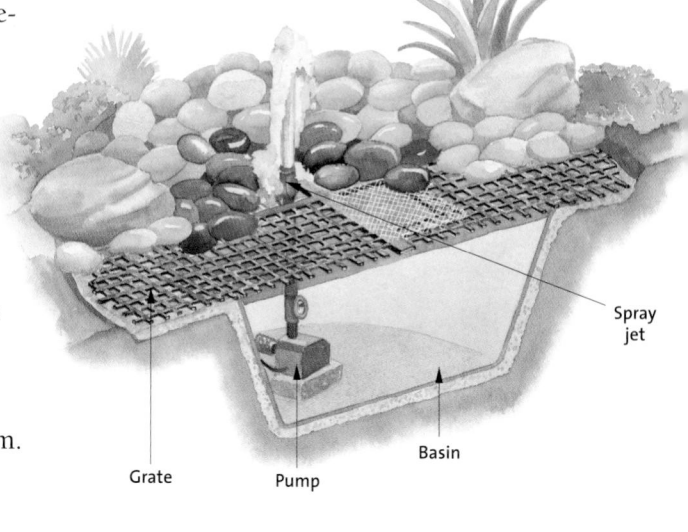

A SPRAY FOUNTAIN

ASSEMBLING A SPRAY FOUNTAIN FROM SMALL ROCKS OR PEBBLES IS RELATIVELY EASY. Besides the rocks, you'll need a pump, a fountain jet, a grate, and an underground basin, as shown below. The basin can be anywhere from 18 to 24 inches wide and should be at least 15 inches deep.

We made our fountain a 4-foot circle, but it can be any shape you like. The spray jet sits just above the top of the stones, as shown. Add a gate valve to fine-tune the flow.

We used a sturdy plastic grate from a pond supplier to hold the rocks. You could also use heavy wire mesh, but it's not as strong. If you're planning to add pebbles that are smaller than the grate openings, add a layer of hardware cloth on top to catch them.

ABOVE: A lively spray jet is the centerpiece of this rock-ringed, ground-level fountain. Besides the rocks and jet, you'll need a sturdy grate, a pump, and a buried basin below. The actual assembly is easy.

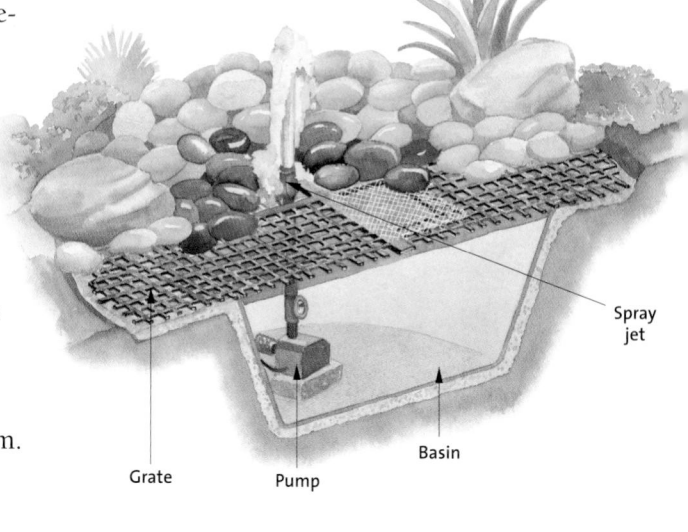

Spray jet

Grate

Pump

Basin

1 **PREPARE THE SITE.** First, mark the outline of your fountain, and remove any sod with a shovel or spade. Then dig a deeper hole for the center basin where your fountain pump will sit, making it slightly wider and deeper than your chosen container.

2 **INSTALL THE BASIN.** Put some sand or gravel into the basin hole and tamp it level. Place the basin in the hole and check that the rim is level; add or remove sand as needed. To help support the sides, backfill the hole with some of the excavated soil or more sand. Tamp down the sides and check again for level.

3 **ADD THE PUMP AND GRATE.** Place the pump atop a clean brick inside the basin. Take the electrical cable out over the edge of the basin in the direction of a GFCI outlet; for safety, bury it in PVC conduit.

Place the grate over the basin, making sure it overlaps the edges by at least 6 inches on all sides. Cut out an access hole big enough to put your hand through comfortably, so you can reach the pump to adjust the water flow or clear the filter screen. Place a square piece of mesh over the cutout, large enough not to sag through the hole once it's covered with rocks.

4 **PLACE THE ROCKS.** Fill the basin with water. Place a few larger stones on the edges of the grate to secure it, then cover the rest of the grate with rocks and pebbles. Plug in the pump and check the jet spray. Adjust the water flow if necessary to ensure that the spray looks the way you want it to—and to be sure the water drips back into the basin.

A WALL FOUNTAIN

In this courtyard garden, water gently splashes from the mouth of a terra-cotta fountain mask into a shallow basin fringed with foliage.

THE BEST WALL FOUNTAINS SEEM TO SPOUT WATER AS IF FROM A HIDDEN SPRING. Though building one from scratch can be tricky, there's a shortcut: Buy a premade fountain mask and basin of your choice, and then take advantage of an existing wall or fence. Water falls from mask to basin, where it recirculates to the top via a small submersible pump and some vinyl tubing.

WATERWAYS

Here, the wisteria growing up and over the brick wall hides the water supply tubing, but any sort of vining plant, or even a trellis placed against the wall, will serve the same purpose. Alternatively, you can run the tubing up the back of the wall or fence and through a hole drilled with a long bit. Our mask hangs on a 3-inch metal dowel inserted in the brick.

Be sure your basin is watertight. The interior of this basin was coated with a sealing agent; a piece of flexible liner could also serve the purpose.

1 **PREP THE MASK.** First, place the mask facedown on a soft surface. Glue several pieces of cork to the back of the mask to lift it far enough from the wall to allow the tubing to run behind it. With a masonry bit, drill a hole up at a 45-degree angle halfway through the back of the mask, directly above the water-spout hole.

2 **THREAD THE TUBING.** Cut a piece of vinyl tubing that's long enough to wind down the wall to reach the basin. Slide an elbow fitting into one end of the tubing. Cut a second piece of tubing, connect it to the other end of the fitting, and push it through the back of the mask's waterspout hole.

3 **HANG THE MASK.** Using a masonry bit, drill a hole 1½ inches deep at a 45-degree angle down into the brick wall where you'll hang the mask. Slide half of a 3-inch metal dowel into the hole. Hang the mask on the wall by sliding it over the other half of the dowel.

4 **CONNECT THE PUMP.** With mask in place, lead the tubing down the wall, concealing it behind vines or lattice. Slide the other end of the tubing over the pump outlet; place the pump in the basin. Fill the basin with water. Plug the pump into a suitable GFCI-protected electrical outlet.

waterfalls and streams

LIKE FOUNTAINS, FALLS AND STREAMS BRING THE
SOUNDS AND SIGHTS OF FLOWING WATER TO YOUR
GARDEN. A MODERN POOL PUMP IS THE KEY—IT TAKES
THE WATER FROM THE BOTTOM AND SHOOTS IT BACK
TO THE TOP, WHERE IT FALLS AGAIN AND AGAIN. BUILD
YOUR WATERFALL WITH OR WITHOUT A POOL. ADD
ROCKS AND BOULDERS TO SUIT YOUR TASTE.

WATERFALL BASICS

THE SPELL OF FLOWING WATER IS SO STRONG THAT PEOPLE TRAVEL HUNDREDS OF MILES TO SEE A WATERFALL. How do you bring some of that magic home? By paying close attention to shape and scale, it's possible to build a bustling waterfall from even a tiny volume of water.

Basically, the idea is to place two or more pools at different heights so that they appear to have been formed by nature. The upper pool is usually the smaller of the two, just large enough to achieve a robust flow of water. A pump gathers water from the lower pool and sends it back to the top via pipes or tubing. Small sites can dispense with the upper pool, but keep things in scale: A torrential fall with its source mysteriously placed midway up a fence won't look credible.

Obviously, a waterfall requires a slope. Hilly sites are a plus. Or use the soil excavated from a garden pool to form the fall's foundation. Most falls are sealed with flexible liners and rimmed with rocks set in mortar. For details, see pages 88–89.

Wide, short falls set a leisurely pace down the rock-lined stream. This water feature begins as a simple shelf sliding toward the pool at top. Metal coyotes stand watch.

FACING PAGE: Ferns, hostas, and hydrangeas border a handmade rock waterfall. Instead of one broad plunge, this fall features tiny cascades formed by small, sharp stones.

The placement of rocks is what really determines your fall's character. Irregular rocks in the center of the channel create a rapids. A big boulder at the base froths up the water even more. An overhang of several inches is best for a curtain effect; some designers add an acrylic lip to keep water from dribbling down the rock face (the acrylic is invisible unless viewed up close). Pinching in the sides of the fall compresses the water, forcing it into a thicker curtain. Gaps, grooves, and other irregularities in the lip create unique patterns. For a booming sound, dig a deep and rather narrow hole into which the water can fall directly.

The key is experimentation—moving one rock here, another there—until the waterfall looks and sounds right. What better excuse to kick off your shoes, roll up your pant legs, and be a kid again for a few hours?

RIGHT: Multiple falls and streams crisscross through waving irises and stacked flagstone edgings, flanking a perfect sitting area up top.

Three tall strands of water tumble through an artful assemblage of small and large rocks. It's hard to tell how the rocks are held in place—what looks like dirt is actually concrete mixed with earth-colored dye.

You don't need a huge, steep space for a waterfall. Small-scale falls can begin with a simple stream, perhaps hidden by plantings in a back corner of your lot. To get the most from a minimal flow, create a single, flat shelf lip, as shown here.

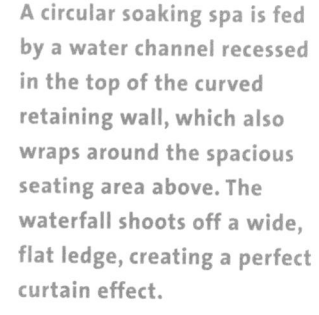

A circular soaking spa is fed by a water channel recessed in the top of the curved retaining wall, which also wraps around the spacious seating area above. The waterfall shoots off a wide, flat ledge, creating a perfect curtain effect.

LEFT: Today's garden designs often blur the distinction between swimming pools and water features. This waterfall tumbles down boulders, then moves in a shallow sheet across the flagstone coping and into the pool. RIGHT: An architectural waterfall shoots through an opening in a backyard retaining wall. Not only does the wall provide an ample drop, but the fall's source can be hidden behind it.

In a hot, dry climate, water is a liquid asset. On this patio, a recirculating waterfall plunges into a semicircular spa. The splashing sounds mask noise from a busy street nearby.

DESIGNING A STREAM

STREAMS ARE AS VARIED AS ANY OF NATURE'S CREATIONS, RANGING FROM TINY TRICKLES TO BOOM- ING RAPIDS. There are rushing, rock-bound moun- tain torrents; zigzagging brooks in upland meadows; and wide, lazy stretches through farm valleys.

ABOVE: Twin stream strands weave through beautiful plantings on their way to the same place: a lily-filled garden pond. Small cascades keep the flow moving toward the pond and add interest.

Although an "architectural" stream (see pages 86–87) might be walled with brick, stone, stucco, or concrete, the classic "natural" stream is formed from strips of flexible liner, overlaid with smooth stones or pea gravel. Loose-aggregate concrete also adds a pebblelike effect.

A natural stream ought to provide the kind of flow that your property can handle easily. Unless your stream bur- bles mysteriously out of the ground, the rushing water usually has a water- fall as its source. An architectural

stream typically issues from either a spray jet or a wall-mounted outlet. In any case, the water must be pumped from the end of the stream (perhaps where it flows into a pool) back to the head, where it begins its journey again.

Though we think of a stream as flowing downhill, most garden streams work best if laid out flat enough to retain some water when the pump isn't running. To negotiate a steeper slope, lower each level section as a unit, connecting sections with small cascades or falls.

Vary the water flow by changing the width and direction of the stream and by placing rocks in it to redirect the current. Straight runs move water quickly; curves slow it down. Water speed will also pick up as the streambed narrows, then slow down as it widens. It's best to build a deeper channel than you think you'll need: Seasonal runoff can flood low banks.

Dry creek beds comprising variably sized smooth rocks suggest the presence of water without even the minimal maintenance demands of other water features. These "creeks" work well in desert regions, but they shine in any climate when they're placed in wet areas to direct seasonal runoff. For details, see pages 90–91.

LEFT: This small-scale stream flows from lush plantings just around the corner—the hidden source could be as simple as a pipe end or small holding pool. RIGHT: A stone-lined stream winds calmly through the landscape, defining the planting and use areas. The arched bridge is a classic addition.

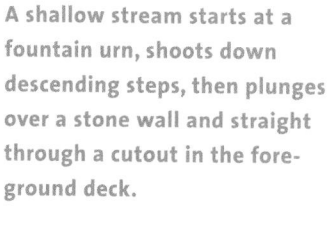

A shallow stream starts at a fountain urn, shoots down descending steps, then plunges over a stone wall and straight through a cutout in the foreground deck.

TOP RIGHT: If you lack water, go for illusion. A dry creek can add the fluid look of water to your landscape while offering great planting options. Here, gray-barked aspen trees and sunny yellow daylilies frame the rocky bed. BOTTOM RIGHT: A more modern dry creek, formed from blue river rocks, snakes through a field of flagstones, adding interest and, of course, saving water.

RIGHT INSET: Underwater lights make a garden stream magical, especially as dusk turns to dark. These lights come in a variety of wattages and bulbs; some have color filters. BELOW: A modern hardscape includes a sleek slate water feature, mixing an angular fountain, stream, and cascade with vibrant colors.

NUTS AND BOLTS

WATERFALLS AND STREAMS POSE SOME UNIQUE TECHNICAL AND DESIGN CONSIDERATIONS. In the technical department, the number-one concern is waterproofing. When it comes to aesthetics, only creative experimentation will reveal the most pleasing sights and sounds. Both waterfalls and streams benefit from tasteful border plantings. For details, see Chapter 4, "Water Gardens."

Waterfall Parts

The drawing below shows an overview of one well-made waterfall. The typical starting point is either a natural incline or the mound of subsoil excavated for a garden pool—perhaps augmented by a retaining wall, sandbags, or other filler material. The entire face of the falls must be sealed to keep water from escaping and to prevent dirt from washing into the lower pool.

Ready-made waterfalls for easy installation are sold by pump and fountain manufacturers. Some rigid shells come with small spillways attached. You can also buy falls formed from simulated rock that almost appear realistic. Viewed from across the yard, these falls may fly, but they don't invite close scrutiny.

Want to build your own? For a waterproof channel, use a flexible liner, a fiberglass shell, a series of spill pans, free-form concrete, or a combination of the above. The team of plastic liner and mortar is favored by many pros. Hide the edges of the channels with natural stones and planting, and use rocks and pebbles to fine-tune the flow. Remember that your waterfall should look good when it's turned off, too.

You'll need a submersible or external pump (see pages 32–33) to move water from the bottom pool or holding basin back to the top, where gravity will send it on its way again.

Fiberglass waterfall

ANATOMY OF A WATERFALL

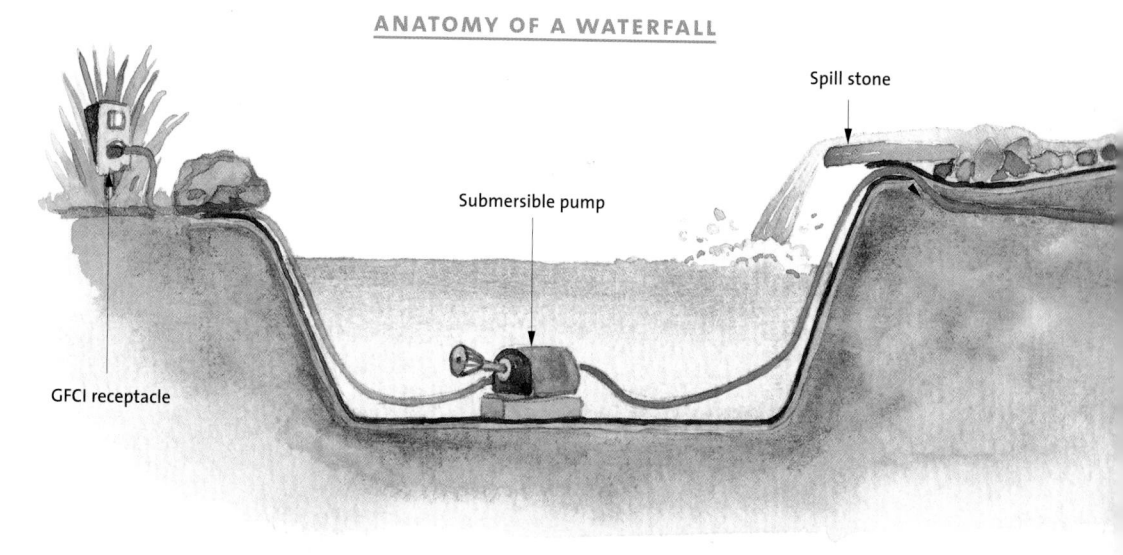

Spill stone

Submersible pump

GFCI receptacle

Fountain spray jets are usually designed for a specific pressure, but waterfalls are more subjective. To choose a pump for a small waterfall, measure the vertical distance from the water level to the top of the fall. Then, using a garden hose, start a flow of water from the top that approximates the volume of water you want. Collect this water in a 5-gallon bucket for a specified time (30 seconds or a minute), multiply the results to get gallons per hour, and compare that figure with the manufacturer's performance data.

When sizing a pump for a large system, it's best to hook up a temporary pump to a 1½-inch hose or the finished plumbing. Your pump should be able to recycle an adequate flow to any filter system (see pages 34–35), so figure in this load as well. If necessary, add a second pump for the filter.

No matter how powerful your pump is, you'll need a large pipe to get a large flow. Be sure that the bottom reservoir or holding pool can hold all the water in the system when the waterfall is off—or install a one-way check valve (see page 37) to keep some water in the pipes when the pump is shut off. A gate valve allows you to fine-tune your fall's flow.

These days, you'll also find a growing list of prefab waterfall boxes and pump chambers, like those shown at right. Both items are great for creating "pondless" waterfalls and streams. For more information, see page 90.

Prefab waterfall box

Pondless pump chamber

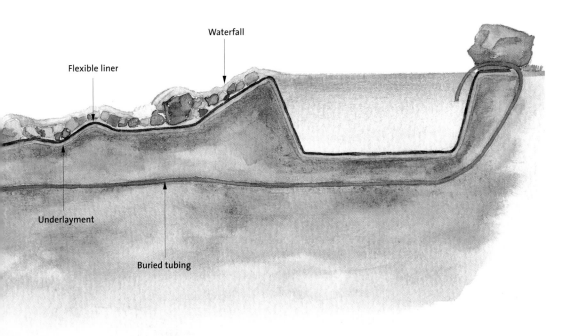

Waterfall

Flexible liner

Underlayment

Buried tubing

A Pondless Waterfall

Pondless falls and streams are all the rage, and for good reason: They fit in small spaces, they're safer for children and pets, and they're easy to care for.

The key to a pondless design is an underground basin or reservoir that takes the place of the lower holding pool. A pump in this reservoir powers the water back up to the falls through a supply pipe. Water flows over the falls at the top, down the stream to the base, disappears into the ground through the rocks, and is recirculated.

The drawing below shows a waterfall box (see page 89) at the top with a built-in biological filter, plus a lidded pump chamber or vault that keeps rocks and dirt out of the pump. A check valve (see page 37) prevents water in the pipe from draining back into the reservoir when the pump is turned off; thus, the reservoir need not be large enough to hold all the water in the system. The reservoir is filled with large cobbles or rocks, then topped with a thin layer of decorative pebbles.

Pondless kits are available from pond suppliers or through the Internet. But you can also make one from scratch, using a heavy-duty grate and flexible liner. It's essentially a bigger version of the fountain shown on pages 72–73. One advantage of this option is that you don't need as large a reservoir—you won't be filling it with rocks.

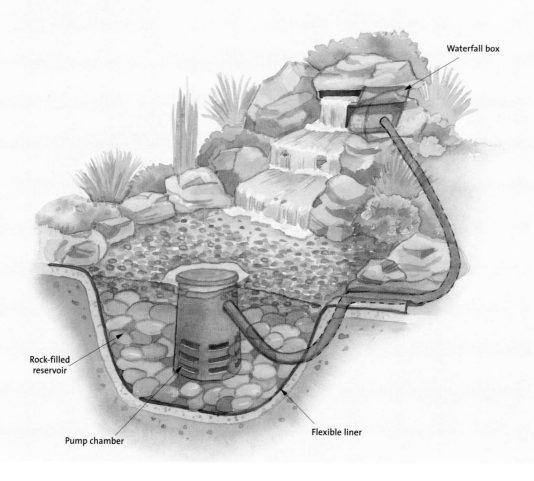

Waterfall box

Rock-filled
reservoir

Flexible liner

Pump chamber

Stream Components

Streams share many construction
details with both waterfalls and
pools—in fact, they typically begin
with a small falls and end in a holding pool.

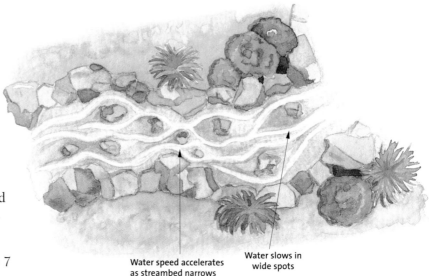

To plan a stream, lay out a hose or
rope in the general course you want
the stream to take. Be sure the proposed
channel can handle the maximum flow
from your pump, plus some additional
natural runoff. A finished depth of 3 to 7
inches works well—anything deeper requires
a lot of water. The slope should be mild; a
series of steps, joined by small, dammed cascades, keeps water from running
off too quickly and retains some when the pump is switched off. Usually, a
drop of 1 inch every 5 to 10 feet is about right.

Water speed accelerates
as streambed narrows

Water slows in
wide spots

SHAPING A STREAM

Flexible liner is an ideal material for streams. You can use one piece of
liner for the entire project or patch one or more pieces together. (Just be sure
to use the tape or glue recommended for the liner you choose.) To find out
how wide your liner should be, first determine the depth of the stream, then
figure twice the depth plus at least 2 feet for overlap on each side. Be sure to
choose a pump with enough power to circulate sufficient water for your project (see pages 32–33).

Dry Creek Beds

A dry creek bed is an attractive option for a natural landscape, doubling as a drainage channel
for seasonal runoff. Except for some digging,
it's easy to build one. You won't need a liner,
though a layer of landscape fabric can help
keep weeds in check. If extra drainage is
required, bury 4-inch perforated drainpipe in
gravel before laying the landscape fabric. Then
add larger rocks along the edges and smaller
stones inside the channel. Border plantings
complete the picture. For a closer look, see the
project on pages 98–99.

Gravel   Landscape fabric

Perforated
drainpipe

DRY CREEK BED

SMALL SCALE, BIG SPLASH

YOU DON'T NEED A HUGE SPACE—OR A LOT OF SKILL—TO BUILD A PLEASING WATERFALL. (You will, of course, need some strength for lifting and digging!) Your falls could be as simple as some stacked, flat flagstones at one end of a small pool (see page 47), with a hidden outlet pipe among the rocks. On the other hand, if you want a large-scale feature, see pages 94–97.

This project fits in between. It measures 13 feet by 6 feet. A pump and skimmer (see page 35) sit on an angle at lower left, a waterfall box (page 89) is at the opposite end. The pebbly beach attracts wading birds.

Here's how to shape the falls. For tips on building the pond, see pages 44–47. Or, if you don't want a pond at all, opt for a so-called "pondless water-fall," as shown on page 90.

A small waterfall flows from a corner of this garden into the rock- and pebble-lined pond. A hidden pump powers water back up to the top.

1. **FIRST, DO SOME DIGGING.** Use a hose to try out different pond shapes and falls placement. Once you've committed to the final layout, mark the outline with bright spray paint.

   Next, use a shovel to excavate the soil for the holding pool. If you wish, pile up some of this soil to form a slope, at the top of which the falls will begin. Shape this slope and water channel, using rocks, concrete blocks, or sandbags as needed to give it a steplike effect. Dig a hole in the slope for the waterfall box and place it now (see page 95 for directions).

2. **INSTALL A LINER.** With padded underlayment in place, line both hole and sloping water channel with a flexible EPDM liner. Place the folded liner at the waterfall end, then unfold it toward the pond (a two-person job for large ponds). Adjust the liner to follow the contours of the pond. Leave the edges untrimmed until after the pond is filled with water.

3. **PLACE LARGE ROCKS.** The toughest part of a falls project is getting any big boulders into place, and you may need help. Dig out beds for large rocks if necessary, so you can settle them firmly in the soil. Position these rocks carefully, making sure not to damage or displace the liner.

   Once the basic structure is complete, place secondary stones, pebbles, and a flagstone waterfall lip, securing them in mortar as needed. Also position some light-colored rocks, which show up better than dark ones, around the edges and bottom of the pond.

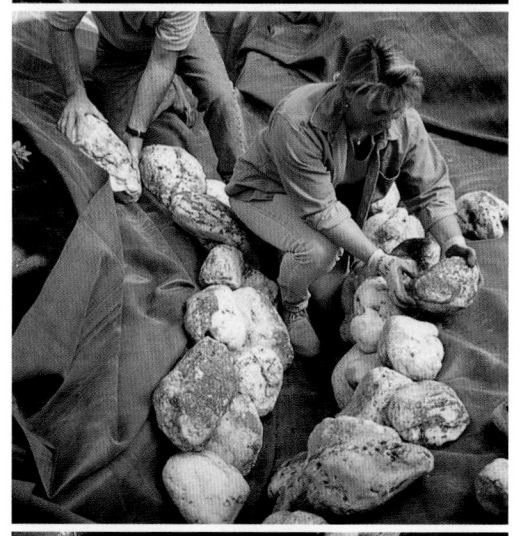

4. **ADD FINISHING TOUCHES.** Use a shovel to scatter gravel among the rocks, then brush small gravel pieces into the spaces between rocks with gloved hands. Toss a few cobbles into the pond, letting them stay where they fall. Hose off all rocks to wash away any dirt, pump the water out of the hole, and refill the pond. Trim the liner, leaving about 12 inches of excess around the edges. Fold under the excess liner (tuck it beneath rocks, if possible); if there's any settling after a few days, you can unfold it.

WATERFALL, STREAM, AND POND

THE BEAUTIFUL WATERFALL-STREAM-POND PROJECT SHOWN HERE IS PRETTY AMBITIOUS. It's also hardware-intensive, featuring a flexible EPDM liner, underlayment, a large pump, pool skimmer, biological filter, check valve, and precast reservoir box. If you want a simpler waterfall design, see page 47 or pages 92–93.

When planning this project, you will probably want to make it visible from inside the house as well as from a patio or deck. And because streams and waterfalls are particularly vulnerable to being dammed by fallen leaves, the presence of trees should also weigh heavily in your choice of location. The sloping ground pictured here, leveling to a sitting area (not shown), is a natural location for this water feature.

Many landscape contractors suggest that a waterfall be constructed no higher than one-third of the vertical distance from the base of the waterfall to the base of the stream. Streambeds are typically 2 to 4 feet wide and 6 to 12 inches deep. For the steeper stream shown here, several twists and turns were added, along with several small waterfalls that spill into shallow pools. The changing directions of the stream add dynamic interest to the water feature, and the small pools will contain much of the stream when the supply pump is shut off.

Installing a pond, stream, and waterfall requires planning and hard work, but the results are well worth it. Such a water feature will quickly form the focal point of your yard.

1 **MARK THE LAYOUT.** Experiment with different shapes for the waterfall, stream, and pond by using a garden hose or rope to mark the outlines. Plan several curves, rapids, and smaller falls en route to the pond. Sketch each new outline and consider your choices over a few days. Once you've decided, mark the final shape with landscaper's spray paint.

2 **PLACE THE WATERFALL BOX.** Find a place at the top of the stream for the waterfall's reservoir box. Dig the hole until the box is at the desired height for the start of the waterfall, then dig down another 6 inches and fill that with packed, crushed rock. At this point, install the water-supply pipe connection and the pipe itself to the back of the box. Use a 4-foot level to confirm that the reservoir is perfectly level side-to-side, and that it's tilted forward until the bubble is about a quarter off-center. Once the reservoir is positioned, backfill around it with the excavated soil and tamp it firmly, checking the level repeatedly to ensure that the reservoir doesn't move.

3 **DIG OUT THE STREAM AND POND.** As you begin digging, adjust the depth and width of the stream to your terrain and your preferences. This homeowner wanted a considerable roar, so a pool 2 feet deep was dug out directly below the falls. Smaller drop-offs and pools were added to the streambed to supplement the volume of water. If you wish, excavate a few deeper holes in the middle and along the sides as you dig your stream. Later, you can fit larger rocks into these holes so that water will swirl around and over them.

continued ▶▶

4 **INSTALL THE SKIMMER BOX.** Next, dig out an area for the skimmer box at the pond's edge. Set the box on a base of crushed rock according to the manufacturer's directions. Be sure that the box is perfectly level from side to side and front to back. Set the pump in the skimmer box. Install the pool liner around the face of the box according to the accompanying directions. Finally, fit a check valve to the pump's discharge side.

5 **BUILD UP THE BORDERS.** Working from the top down, install rocks of varying sizes along the streambed to outline the shape and reinforce the banks. Add more soil as necessary to build up the lower sides of stream curves to prevent running water from washing over. Also deepen the streambed as necessary at sharp curves to keep the water contained. Fill gaps between large rocks with washed drain rock at least 2 inches in diameter. Later, when you place the liner, it will fit over the built-up soil embankments. You'll resettle the larger rocks to anchor the liner, and they'll be an integral part of the stream's edge.

6 **RUN SUPPLY PIPE.** Lay the flexible vinyl pipe (in this case, 2-inch diameter) between the waterfall reservoir and the pump in the skimmer box. The supply pipe can be buried in the streambed or run up the side of the garden, as here, depending on convenience. Bury the pipe 6 inches deep to protect it from damage.

7 **ADD UNDERLAYMENT, THEN THE LINER.** Starting from the top, pull the underlayment across the streambed and pond and fit it to the excavation as you work down the slope. Add extra cushioning over any sharp rocks or roots that could not be removed. Fit the underlayment as smoothly as possible and then install the EPDM liner in the same manner. Folds and wrinkles are unavoidable, but smooth them as best you can.

8 **HIDE THE BOX.** After pulling the stream liner up to the front of the reservoir box and attaching it according to the manufacturer's directions, begin installing rocks around the box to hide it. When possible, mix large and small rocks for a more natural appearance. Place the largest rocks on each side of the box to frame it, then build up the center section. Rocks can be glued to each other and to the liner with pure silicone caulk or black expanding foam, sold at pond-supply outlets. The foam is also useful to fill gaps between large rocks. Once it's injected, press gravel and sand into the foam to disguise it.

9 **FINE-TUNE THE FALLS.** Many waterfall boxes are equipped with a plastic lip to form the waterfall, but for a better appearance, fit a wide, flat rock to the lip and hold it in place with ample amounts of silicone caulk. How far out the stone extends will determine the type of falls you have. For a direct plunge, extend the lip over the pool. Shorten the extension if you want the water to splash down and over the rocks that support the waterfall.

10 **ADD PLANTS.** The last—and best—part of any water garden project is bringing it to life with a selection of plants, shrubs, and flowers. Your choice is wide but will be dictated in part by your climate. For a closer look at plants, see Chapter Four, "Water Gardens."

A DRY CREEK BED

WANT TO ADD THE LOOK OF WATER WITHOUT THE FUSS? Build a dry creek bed that looks as though a rushing stream had deposited the stones and settled them in. The trick to making a pile of rocks look like a streambed is to arrange them along a slight depression. Even more important, construct the creek bed with stones that appear to have been worn smooth by centuries of flowing water. Some should be round, some flat—mix large and small together, just as they would naturally occur in an actual stream. If your dry creek will carry seasonal runoff, consider adding some 4-inch perforated drainpipe down the center (as shown on page 91).

The bed pictured at left took two people only four hours (including shopping time) to complete and cost less than $300. It measures 17 feet long and widens from 1 foot to 5 feet; it's 1 inch deep at the sides and 3 inches at center. To build one like it, you'll need a roll of landscape fabric, some boulders ranging from about 1 to 2 feet across, cobblestones or river rock in varying sizes, and a good supply of pebbles.

You don't need water to suggest its presence in the garden. Why not try a dry creek instead? To make one like this requires a good supply of rock, but only a few hours of time.

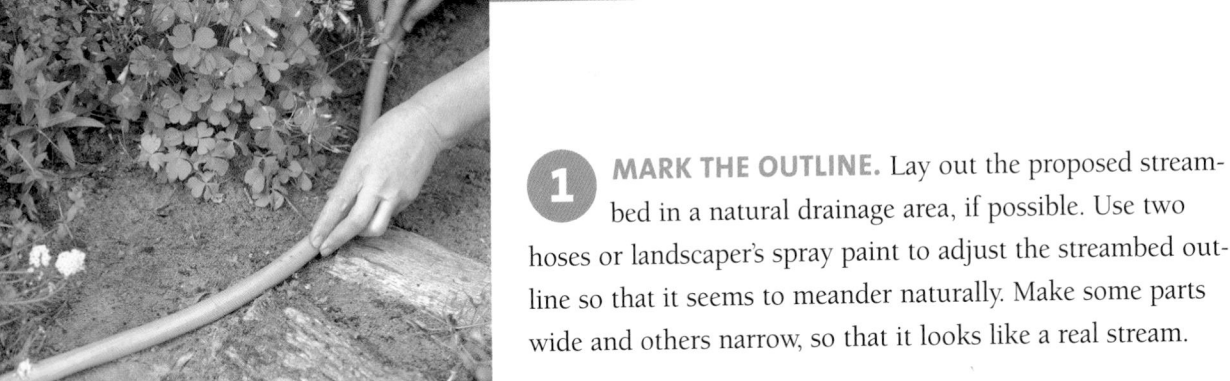

1 MARK THE OUTLINE. Lay out the proposed stream-bed in a natural drainage area, if possible. Use two hoses or landscaper's spray paint to adjust the streambed outline so that it seems to meander naturally. Make some parts wide and others narrow, so that it looks like a real stream.

2 DIG THE STREAMBED. Dig the channel with a spade or shovel, making it deeper in the center. Use excess soil to build berms beside the bed. (If you're planning to add drainpipe, also dig a deeper trench down the center to house it.)

3 LINE THE BED. Lay landscape fabric over the streambed to prevent weeds from sprouting. Fold and pleat the cloth as needed where the stream curves, narrows, and widens. Avoid getting soil on fabric (it can host weeds). Also place any boulders, setting them into depressions dug 1 to 2 inches deep beneath the fabric. Be sure the boulders do not line up in a regimented manner but are spaced naturally.

4 ADD ROCKS AND PEBBLES. Scatter some of the largest cobblestones on top of the fabric, then add a 1-inch layer of pebbles around them. Toss in the remaining large cobbles and finish with the smallest ones. Walk lightly on the bed to settle the stones. As desired, add plants along the sides of the streambed. It's best to use plants native to your area—for example, mix tall grasses with lower flowering shrubs.

CROSSINGS

STREAMS AND PONDS SEEM MADE TO BE CROSSED. After all, who can resist finding out what's on the other side? Crossings also make decorative accents and add new perspectives from which to view your water feature and see plants and fish close up. A crossing may consist of some large rocks conveniently placed in the water, a flat or gently arched bridge, or just two logs with decking formed by stout limbs.

Use stepping stones to cross a pool or stream. Keep the distance between stones close enough to provide safe passage, but try to avoid straight linear arrangements.

Stepping Stones

The simplest way to span a small stream is via large stepping stones set in the water. This is not so much a bridge as an extension of a path. Materials include cast concrete shapes, sliced log rounds, quarried flat stones, and natural boulders. For greater visual interest, stagger the stones. Close spacings are safer and encourage visitors to linger awhile.

In deeper water, mortared brick or stone piers provide solid foundations for stepping stones. A brick pier is shown below. Build one pier for each stone. If you prefer, flat stones can be used instead of bricks.

If you'll be using a flexible liner, decide on a layout early in the planning stage. That way, you can cast the necessary concrete footing for each pier before installing the liner. It's also a good idea to add an extra layer of underlayment to each footing. The footings should be about 4 inches thick and slightly larger than the piers that will rest on them.

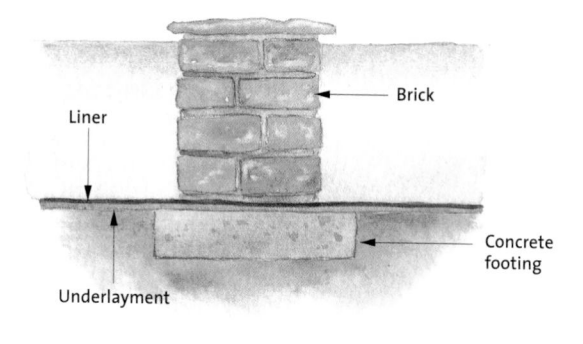

MORTARED BRICK PIER

Brick

Liner

Concrete footing

Underlayment

Bridges

For wide streams and pools, you may need a bridge instead. Plan for one that's 2 to 3 feet wide to promote a sense of security for those who walk across it; a railing is recommended for long bridges or those over deep water.

Three basic bridge-building materials are wood, cast concrete, and quarried stone. Wood is the lightest, least expensive, and most versatile to work with—especially for do-it-yourselfers.

The basic wood bridge shown below right is quite easy to build. It spans up to 8 feet, with 2 by 6 joists spaced 24 inches on center. The design can be customized to fit different needs. To keep it safe, however, you need to make sure the lumber you use does not surpass its allowable spans. Midspan support posts, if they're necessary, can be sunk directly into the bottom of a concrete stream or can be supported by concrete footings below a flexible liner.

If you choose to add railings, a simple yet functional design is shown at bottom right. Posts are made from 4 by 4s, spaced about 4 feet apart, with notches cut in the bottoms to fit over the joists. Attach posts to joists with carriage bolts. Nail a 2 by 4 crosspiece to the posts, then add a 2 by 6 cap rail on top.

Flat bridges should be 6 inches to a foot above the surface of the water; if the distance is greater, the sense of intimacy may be lost. To further blend bridge with stream, arrange stones both on the banks and in the water near the ends of the bridge.

If the prospect of building your own bridge seems too time-consuming or daunting, some garden pool dealers carry ready-built units that can be shipped to your door and assembled in a couple of hours.

This flat wood bridge spans a naturalistic pond. The smoothly rounded river rocks and graceful bog and water plants help soften the edges of the structure.

A BASIC WOOD BRIDGE

2 × 4 or 2 × 6 decking

Concrete footing

2 × 6 joist

2 × 6 cap rail

2 × 4 crosspiece

4 × 4 post

RAILINGS

water
gardens

WANT A NEW CANVAS FOR GARDENING ARTS? WATER
PLANTS RANGE FROM SHOWY LOTUSES AND FLOATING
WATER LILIES TO TINY, INVISIBLE OXYGENATORS. MAR-
GINAL AND BOG PLANTS ADD COLOR AND TEXTURE,
LINKING YOUR POOL TO THE LANDSCAPE. PLANTS ALSO
PROVIDE SHADE AND OXYGEN FOR FISH. HERE'S HOW
TO BECOME A WATER GARDENER.

DESIGNING YOUR WATER GARDEN

GARDENING OPTIONS GROW INSTANTLY WHEN YOU ADD A POOL TO THE LANDSCAPE. From vibrant water lilies and lotuses to small floating plants that form colorful carpets on the water, your choice of pool plants is wide and varied.

Remember that almost all aquatic plants need good sunlight to thrive and bloom. When locating your water garden, try to select a spot that enjoys direct sun for a majority of the day. The most successful water gardens also provide a range of depths throughout the pool, because some plants will grow in several inches of water while others may require several feet.

You'll want to include a few plants that serve specialized functions, such as providing oxygen and helping reduce algae in the pond (see "Oxygenating Plants" on page 107). Beyond that, your goals should be much the same as when you design any other kind of garden: to choose plants that will provide variety and interest throughout the year and to arrange them in a visually pleasing way.

Here's the number-one rule for planning your water garden: Start with restraint. Consider the mature growth of the plants when figuring layout and spacing. A garden sketch is a big help.

To avoid the "jungle" look, arrange your plantings so they'll form the kind of progression or backdrop you'd like (you'll probably want delicate plants up front, for instance, and taller, leafier species in the back). Plan the layout to take advantage of different color schemes and seasons. For example, water hawthorn blooms in winter and provides a punch of color when water lilies die back.

Transitions are also important. To create a graceful link between your pond and the landscape around it, choose border species that are compatible with the plantings in both areas.

Are you planning on adding fish? The right mix and proportion of plants will oxygenate the water, shade it from the hot sun, and provide food for the fish. For details on choosing and raising fish, see Chapter Five, "Goldfish and Koi."

ABOVE: Even a tiny, rock-ringed pool makes a suitable canvas for a floating carpet of plants.
OPPOSITE: This water garden was designed as a backyard wildlife habitat. Besides providing shelter for animals and a water source for birds, Jupiter's beard and sweet alyssum (foreground) supply nectar for butterflies.

PLANTS FOR THE POND

WATER PLANTS COME IN FOUR BASIC TYPES: FLOATING, OXYGENATING, MARGINAL, AND BOG OR BORDER. Here, we take a look at the general characteristics and uses of each category. For photos and descriptions of specific water plants, see pages 110–115. Ready to start planting? Turn to pages 116–119 for strategies and suggestions.

Some pond plants are showstoppers—like these lotuses, which have roots in soil, and large leaves atop the water surface. In season, they shoot stunning blooms, up to 1 foot wide, into the air.

This pond contains a healthy mix of aquatic life: water lilies and other floating plants; marginals, including irises; and oxygenators submerged in the water.

Floating Plants

There are two types of floating plants: those with their roots in the soil and their leaves floating on the surface, such as water lilies and lotuses; and plants such as water hyacinth or water lettuce, whose roots simply float in the water.

Rooted plants, sometimes called "floating-leaf" plants or "semi-floaters," are not only beautiful, but they help keep the pool healthy by providing shade and crowding out competing algae. They don't like heavy turbulence, so plant them away from the splash of a waterfall or fountain.

True floaters get their nutrients directly from the water and don't need soil to grow. Some act as natural filters, soaking up ammonia and other toxins. Most free-floating plants can become invasive, especially in warmer climates, and need to be thinned periodically. Water hyacinth, for example, grew so rapidly when introduced to Florida streams that the plants became a menace to navigation. For this reason, some floaters are banned in certain states. Keep floaters away from koi, since the fish shred the roots, which in turn can clog your pump.

Vibrant, tiered blossoms of primrose enliven this damp, shady bog garden beside a pond.

Oxygenating Plants

These hard workers grow submerged beneath the pool's surface. Although they do not bloom and are rarely seen, they are, nevertheless, indispensable to a balanced water garden. During daylight hours, oxygenators take up carbon dioxide and release oxygen to other plants and to fish in the pond. Oxygenators also provide a spawning area for fish and a handy hiding place for small-fry until they get big enough to fend for themselves.

Some common oxygenators include fanwort, pondweed, and eel grass. They are usually sold in bunches. It's a good idea to choose several types, since their periods of active growth may vary.

ABOVE: Cascades lace through a lushly planted hillside. The nooks and crannies of these rocky falls were first packed with soil, then filled with plants. OPPOSITE: Mexican weeping bamboo forms a sturdy streamside screen in this California garden.

Marginal Plants

Some water plants do best around the pool's margins, with their heads waving in the breeze and their feet in shallow water. Two classic examples are Japanese iris and arrowhead. Most marginal plants prefer water 1 to 6 inches deep. These are the plants that benefit from a separate, adjoining shallow area in your pool or a series of shelves around the edges.

Marginal plants help provide a smooth transition from pool to dry land in both formal and natural garden pools. And because they grow rapidly in water, these plants quickly lend a mature look to a new pond.

Bog Plants

Other plants grow best around the pool's borders, where splashing water keeps the ground moist. These bog plants camouflage the edges of a pool, waterfall, or stream, lending a natural appearance. They also extend the water-plant environment, making the pool look larger or tying it to its sur-roundings. Bog plants—such as primroses, lobelias, and hostas—often come from plant families seen in the garden at large.

Two worthy mentions, not really bog plants but often associated with natu-ral pool settings, are Japanese maple (*Acer palmatum*) and bamboo (available in many varieties).

A GUIDE TO WATER PLANTS

Pondweed

SCORES OF PLANTS ARE AVAILABLE FOR PLANTING IN AND AROUND YOUR POOL. Below, we describe some of the most popular, broken down by basic type: oxygenating, floating-leaf, free-floating, and marginal or bog. Many of these plants can be found at nurseries in your area; all of them, and more, can be ordered by mail or on the Internet.

Which water plants are surefire winners in your microclimate? It's a good idea to ask your local nursery personnel or another pool owner in the neighborhood; or contact a mail-order plant supplier that sells nationwide.

It's fun to choose the plants yourself, but if you'd rather leave the decisions to someone else, consider one of the collections offered by some suppliers. There are different collections suited to different pond sizes (based on surface area). They typically include all the plants needed for a well-balanced pool.

Oxygenating Plants

Canadian pondweed
Elodea canadensis
Description: Tiny, dark green leaves on threadlike, tangled stems. Tiny greenish white flowers in summer. To control it, pinch off old growth or remove excess with a net or rake. **Hardiness:** To –30°F/–34°C. **Planting:** Thrives in cool water. Full sun.

Eel grass
Vallisneria americana
Description: Slender, ribbonlike leaves up to 2 ft. long float beneath the water surface. Long-stalked little flowers float on surface in summer. **Hardiness:** To 20°F/–7°C. **Planting:** Place in shallow, wide pot or tray to allow horizontal growth; new plants form along runners. Best in still water. Full sun.

Fanwort
Cabomba caroliniana
Description: Fan-shaped, feathery, bright green foliage. Small white flowers float on water in summer. **Hardiness:** To –10°F/–23°C. **Planting:** Best in warm, still water. Full sun.

Pondweed
Potamogeton spp.
Description: Many species with translucent, seaweedlike leaves. Tiny flower spikes just above the water surface in summer. Foliage provides food and shelter for fish. **Hardiness:** Some species to –20°F/–29°C. **Planting:** Prefers sun but tolerates some shade.

Fanwort

Floating-Leaf Plants

Lotus
Nelumbo spp.

Description: Available as started plants or as tubers. Big, round, green leaves to 2 ft. across. Fragrant white, cream, pink, red, or yellow flowers to 1 ft. wide stand above foliage in summer. Ornamental woody fruit, perforated like a salt shaker, follows. **Hardiness:** To −30°F/−34°C, but best in warm climates. **Planting:** In water to 24 in. deep for larger varieties, to 9 in. deep for smaller ones. Rhizomes are brittle, easily damaged. Full sun.

Water poppy

Water clover

Water clover
Marsilea spp.

Description: Ferns with foliage like that of four-leaf clover; floats on surface forming carpet. Thin as necessary. **Hardiness:** To −10°F/−23°C. **Planting:** In water to 12 in. deep. Also grows in moist soil, standing erect to 1 ft. tall. Can become invasive; best in pots. Sun or shade.

Water hawthorn
Aponogeton distachyus

Description: Long-stemmed, straplike, bright green leaves to 8 in. long. Fragrant white flowers 1¼ in. wide in two-branched clusters above the water from spring to early fall in cold climates, year-round in mild ones. May disappear in summer heat. **Hardiness:** To 23°F/−5°C. **Planting:** In water to 24 in. deep. Full sun or part shade.

Water lily
Nymphaea spp.

Description: Round leaves, deeply notched where stem is attached. Available in hardy and tropical varieties. Spectacular flowers in white, yellow, copper, pink, or red; tropical varieties also available in blue and purple. For additional details, see page 119. **Hardiness:** Hardy types to −40°F/−40°C; tropical types to 30°F/−1°C. **Planting:** In water to 24 in. deep for hardy types; to 12 in. deep for tropical types. Full sun (there are some shade-tolerant varieties).

Water lily

Water poppy
Hydrocleys nymphoides

Description: Long, trailing stems with heart-shaped, shiny, dark green leaves to 3 in. long. Bowl-shaped 3-in. yellow flowers just above the water in summer. **Hardiness:** To 30°F/−1°C. **Planting:** In water to 24 in. deep. Full sun or part shade.

Water snowflake

Water snowflake, floating heart
Nymphoides spp.

Description: Most types have round leaves to about 3 in. across, sometimes mottled with brown. Small, fringed yellow or white flowers like little water lilies held above the water in summer. **Hardiness:** Some species to −10°F/−23°C. **Planting:** In water to 24 in. deep. Full sun.

Free-Floating Plants

Fairy moss, mosquito plant
Azolla caroliniana

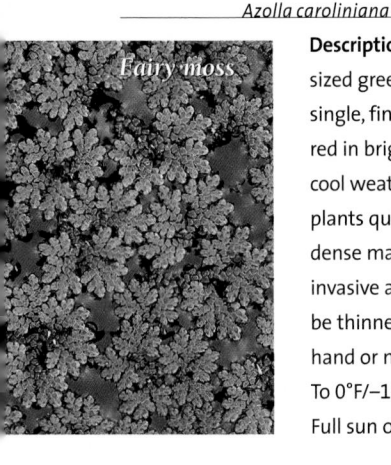

Fairy moss

Description: Dime-sized green fern with a single, fine root. Turns red in bright sun or cool weather. A few plants quickly form a dense mat. Can be invasive and needs to be thinned out by hand or net. **Hardiness:** To 0°F/−18°C. **Planting:** Full sun or part shade.

Frogbit
Hydrocharis morsus-ranae

Description: Rounded, shiny green leaves to 2 in. across, like little lily pads. Small, bowl-shaped white flowers with yellow centers in summer. **Hardiness:** To 0°F/−18°C. **Planting:** Prefers calm, shallow water. Full sun.

Frogbit

Water hyacinth

Water fern
Salvinia minima

Description: Fern with two rounded, stiffly hairy, $1/2$-in. floating leaves like miniature lily pads; emerald green in shade but often brownish in full sun. Submerged, modified third leaf acts as a root. **Hardiness:** To 30°F/−1°C. **Planting:** Prefers still water. Full sun or part shade.

Water hyacinth
Eichhornia crassipes

Description: Rounded, shiny green leaves to about 5 in. across held just above the water by air-filled stems. Pale lavender blue flower spikes to 6 in. tall in warmer climates in summer. Foot-long feathery roots form spawning areas for fish. **Hardiness:** To 10°F/−12°C. **Planting:** Full sun.

Water lettuce
Pistia stratiotes

Description: Velvety green, 6-in. rosettes, like little heads of looseleaf lettuce. Can form a mat several feet wide by summer's end. Long, trailing roots turn from white to purple to black; good fish cover. **Hardiness:** To 30°F/−1°C. **Planting:** Prefers calm, shallow water. Needs midday shade in hot climates.

Water lettuce

Marginal and Bog Plants

Arrowhead
Sagittaria spp.

Description: Big green leaves shaped like arrowheads. White, saucerlike summer flowers. *S. latifolia* has broad leaves, *S. sagittifolia* 'Flore Pleno' *(S. japonica)* has narrow leaves, double flowers. **Hardiness:** To –20°F/–29°C. **Planting:** In moist soil or in water to 6 in. deep. Full sun or part shade.

Canna hybrids

Description: Large, lance-shaped leaves may be rich green, bronzy red, or variegated. Showy flower spikes are red, orange, yellow, pink, cream, white, or bicolored in summer, fall. **Hardiness:** To 0°F/–18°C. **Planting:** In moist, rich soil or in water to 6 in. deep. Best in a sunny, hot spot.

Canna

Cardinal flower
Lobelia cardinalis

Description: Erect, single-stemmed plant with bronzy green leaves set directly on stem. Spikes of 1-in. scarlet tubular flowers in summer. **Hardiness:** To –40°F/–40°C. **Planting:** In moist soil. Tolerates water to 2 in. deep. Full sun or part shade.

Cattail

Cattail
Typha spp.

Description: Long, swordlike or linear leaves. Cylindrical brown flower heads in summer. Pygmy cattail *(T. minima)*, 1 to 1½ ft. tall, is best for small ponds. Other species need more space. **Hardiness:** Some species to –40°F/–40°C. **Planting:** In moist soil or in water to 6 in. deep for *T. minima,* 12 in. deep for larger species. Invasive; best in pots. Full sun or part shade.

Daylily
Hemerocallis hybrids

Description: Evergreen, semievergreen, and deciduous types, all with arching, sword-shaped leaves; lilylike spring or summer flowers in yellow, orange, rusty red, pink, purple, apricot, buff, or cream, often with contrasting eyes or stripes. Some types bloom again later; others bloom throughout warm weather. **Hardiness:** To –40°F/–40°C. **Planting:** In moist, rich soil or in water to 4 in. deep. Full sun; needs part shade in hottest climates.

Elephant's ear, taro
Colocasia esculenta

Description: Succulent stalks hold huge (up to 3 ft. long), heart-shaped green leaves from spring through fall. Some forms have black or purple stalks and foliage. **Hardiness:** To 20°F/–7°C. **Planting:** In moist, rich soil or in water to 10 in. deep. Best in warm, filtered sun.

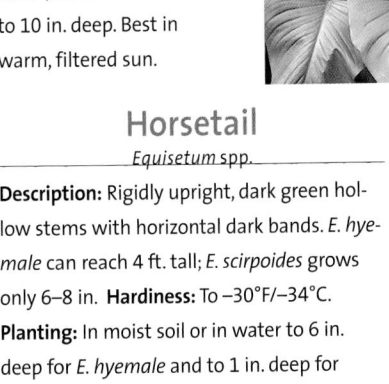

Elephant's ear

Horsetail
Equisetum spp.

Description: Rigidly upright, dark green hollow stems with horizontal dark bands. *E. hyemale* can reach 4 ft. tall; *E. scirpoides* grows only 6–8 in. **Hardiness:** To –30°F/–34°C. **Planting:** In moist soil or in water to 6 in. deep for *E. hyemale* and to 1 in. deep for *E. scirpoides.* Invasive; best in pots. Full sun or part shade.

Daylily

Primrose

Pickerel weed, pickerel rush
Pontederia cordata

Description: Long-stalked, glossy green, heart-shaped leaves to 10 in. long stand well above water. Blue flower spikes from late spring to fall. **Hardiness:** To −40°F/−40°C. **Planting:** In water to 6 in. deep. Full sun or light shade.

Primrose
Primula spp.

Description: Green foliage rosettes topped by flowers in spring, early summer. Moisture lovers include species with tiered blossoms: *P. japonica* (purple with yellow eye, white, or pink); *P. prolifera* (fragrant yellow); and *P. pulverulenta* (red to red-purple). *P. florindae* has clusters of fragrant, nodding yellow blooms. **Hardiness:** Some species to −20°F/−29°C. **Planting:** In moist, rich, acid soil. Part or full shade; can take full sun in cool-summer climates.

Iris

Hosta spp.

Description: Main feature is a broad mound of overlapping leaves, which are rounded to lance-shaped, shiny or dull, smooth or textured, in shades of green, chartreuse, blue, or gray. Many selections are edged or marked with a contrasting color. Thin spikes of lavender or white trumpet-shaped flowers in summer. Makes a great backdrop for showier pond plants. **Hardiness:** To −40°F/−40°C. **Planting:** In moist, rich soil. Part or full shade.

Iris spp.

Description: Swordlike green leaves and showy flowers. Water-loving species include blue flag, *I. versicolor* (violet-blue blooms); Japanese iris, *I. ensata* (purple, violet, pink, rose, red, white); *I. laevigata* (violet, magenta, white); and yellow flag, *I. pseudacorus* (bright yellow, ivory, pale yellow). Also Siberian irises (purple, blue, white, cream, yellow, pink, wine red) and Louisiana irises (wide range of colors), derived from several species. **Hardiness:** Some species to −50°F/−46°C. **Planting:** In moist, rich soil or in water to 6 in. deep (to 10 in. deep for *I. pseudacorus*). Siberian irises won't tolerate standing water, and *I. ensata* tolerates it only during growing season. Full sun or light shade.

Marsh marigold
Caltha palustris

Description: Rounded, glossy green, toothed leaves 2–7 in. wide. Clusters of 2-in. bright yellow flowers in late winter, early spring. There are white-flowered and double-flowered forms. **Hardiness:** To −30°F/−34°C. **Planting:** In moist soil or in water to 6 in. deep. Full sun or part shade.

Parrot feather
Myriophyllum aquaticum

Description: Whorls of feathery, emerald green leaves on trailing stems to 6 ft. long; tips emerge from water. Roots provide a good spawning area for fish. Also grown as an oxygenator. **Hardiness:** To −10°F/−23°C. **Planting:** In water to 12 in. deep. Obtains nutrients from the water, so can be planted in gravel. Full sun or part shade.

Parrot feather

Rush
Juncus spp.

Description: Clump of leaflike, cylindrical green or gray stems with tiny flowers near stem tips. Most are grown for vertical form; corkscrew rush (*J. effusus* 'Spiralis') features twisting stems. **Hardiness:** Some species to −30°F/−34°C. **Planting:** In moist soil or in water to 4 in. deep. Full sun or part shade.

Sweet flag

Sedge

Sweet flag
Acorus spp.

Description: Fans of grasslike leaves resemble miniature iris; may be entirely green or striped with cream or white. Some dwarf forms are less than 1 ft. tall. **Hardiness:** Some species to −30°F/−34°C. **Planting:** In moist, rich soil or in water to 6 in. deep (to 2 in. deep for dwarfs). Full sun or part shade.

Umbrella grass, umbrella palm
Cyperus spp.

Description: Umbrellalike, leafy green whorls atop triangular stems. Choices include *C. alternifolius,* to 3 ft. tall, and *C. papyrus,* a dramatic accent 6–10 ft. tall. **Hardiness:** Some species to 20°F/−7°C. **Planting:** In moist, rich soil or in water to 6 in. deep for larger species; or to 2 in. deep for smaller types. Full sun or part shade.

Sedge
Carex spp.

Description: Hardy, grasslike perennial with colorful leaves that provide texture year-round. Up to 2,000 species that vary in height from 6 inches to 5 feet. Color and leaf form also vary. **Hardiness:** To −20°F/−29°C. **Planting:** In moist soil or in water to 4 in. deep. Leaf color most intense in full sun.

Water canna
Thalia dealbata

Description: Long-stalked, paddle-shaped, bluish green leaves to 1$^1/_2$ ft. long. Foliage topped by violet-blue flower spikes to 8 in. long in summer. **Hardiness:** To −10°F/−23°C. **Planting:** In moist soil or in water to 24 in. deep. Full sun.

Water hyssop
Bacopa monnieri

Description: Sprawling ground cover with succulent, $^3/_4$-in. green leaves. Small white or pale blue flowers, spring into fall. **Hardiness:** To 10°F/−12°C. **Planting:** In moist soil at edge of slow-moving stream or pond. Will often extend shoots to float in water and send down long roots. Full sun or part shade.

Umbrella grass

PLANTING TECHNIQUES

WATER PLANTS PURCHASED FROM A LOCAL NURSERY OR POND SUPPLIER ARE SOMETIMES SUITABLY POTTED UP and ready for placing in the water. If they're not, you'll need to prepare them, as you would any mail-order plants that arrive bare-root or in very small pots. Here's the lowdown on choosing pots for ponds. For step-by-step planting pointers, see page 118.

All about Containers

Most water gardeners plant in pots, even when it's possible to do otherwise. Not only do the pots restrain vigorous plants, but they simplify maintenance—you just lift the pots out when it's time to divide the plants or clean the pool. Floating plants don't really need rooting, but a container will help isolate and contain these sometimes invasive species. Small pots also help control the spread of oxygenators.

Pond owners use all kinds of containers: plastic nursery pots, wire-mesh baskets, wooden crates and boxes, and even plastic dishpans and buckets. Various containers that allow water and gases to circulate are made especially for water plants. In general, try to choose larger pots over smaller ones, as long as you can pick them up when they're filled with wet soil. Large pots provide more growing room, and they're less likely to tip over.

Plan to line perforated containers with fabric, such as untreated burlap, to keep the soil from escaping into the water. You'll also need a supply of pea gravel to cover the soil and hold it in place. Or, if you plan to raise goldfish or koi, use larger river rocks to keep the fish from uprooting your plants. Some fish suppliers sell special planting bags that surround the entire container and protect the plant roots and crowns from fish.

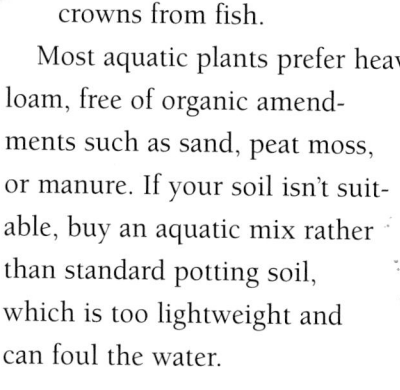

Pots for ponds

Most aquatic plants prefer heavy loam, free of organic amendments such as sand, peat moss, or manure. If your soil isn't suitable, buy an aquatic mix rather than standard potting soil, which is too lightweight and can foul the water.

Aquatic planting mix

Tub Gardens

If you don't have space for a full-scale water garden, don't despair—instead, plant a tub garden. You'll need only a few springtime hours and some simple ingredients: a suitable container, a sunny site, some water plants, and maybe a few fish to help keep the pool clean.

For help with buying or building containers, see pages 10–11 and page 40. Because a water-filled container is quite heavy, it makes good sense to set up your tub garden in its permanent location. You may prefer to place it on garden ground rather than on a deck or patio; the pool will have to be drained occasionally, and there's always some chance of seepage.

As you evaluate possible sites, remember that it's important to provide plenty of sunshine. Most aquatic plants need at least 4 to 6 hours of full sun daily. Keep in mind, too, that your water garden should complement its surroundings. You may want to locate the pool where it will reflect color from blooming trees and flowers, for example.

With the exception of plants that simply float free on the water surface, root aquatic plants before placing them in the tub. Submerge the planted pots in the tub, positioning them so the tops of the pots are under water. To raise plants to the proper height, set up pedestals (made from bricks or overturned pots) on the bottom of the pool.

Add a goldfish or two, or some mosquito fish, to keep the water free of insects—or try a couple of mosquito rings instead (see page 35). A tiny fountain jet, driven by a submersible pump, provides visual interest as well as aeration.

Once a year, drain the pool and scrub it out thoroughly with a mixture of four parts water to one part household bleach.

Listed below are a few popular tub plants. For more complete descriptions and planting details, see pages 110–115.

Arrowhead *(Sagittaria latifolia)*
Cardinal flower *(Lobelia cardinalis)*
Horsetail *(Equisetum hyemale)*
Lotus *(Nelumbo)*
Japanese iris *(Iris ensata)*
Pygmy cattail *(Typha minima)*
Umbrella grass *(Cyperus alternifolius)*
Water hyacinth *(Eichhornia crassipes)*
Water hawthorn *(Aponogeton distachyus)*
Water lily *(Nymphaea)*

Planting in the Pond

Some water plants have specific depth requirements (see pages 110–115); simply adjust the height of their containers with bricks or concrete blocks, as shown below. Just be careful not to tear the pool liner. Some water plants need to be closer to the surface when young; they can be lowered to their more permanent depth after they've become established. Simply build them up on bricks or blocks, then gradually remove the blocks as the plants mature.

Water lilies and some other water plants are not at all fond of heavy turbulence, so be sure to locate them out of the direct splash-zone of a fountain or waterfall.

Creating a Bog Garden

Normally, gardeners fight for adequate drainage of their plants. In a bog garden, though, you try to retain water. The splash from the pool will do for many plants, or you can simply set a pot in the water, with its lip just above the surface. Another option is to backfill a border area with heavy soil and gravel.

More formal bog gardens can be designed by running an overflow pipe from the pool to the bog and/or using a flexible liner below the garden to retain water. You won't need an expensive liner—in fact, you'll probably be punching holes in it so that some water can drain off. Wherever your bog meets the pool, build a rock dam, as shown below, and line its face with landscape fabric to keep bog soil from filtering into the pool water.

PLANTING PROFILE

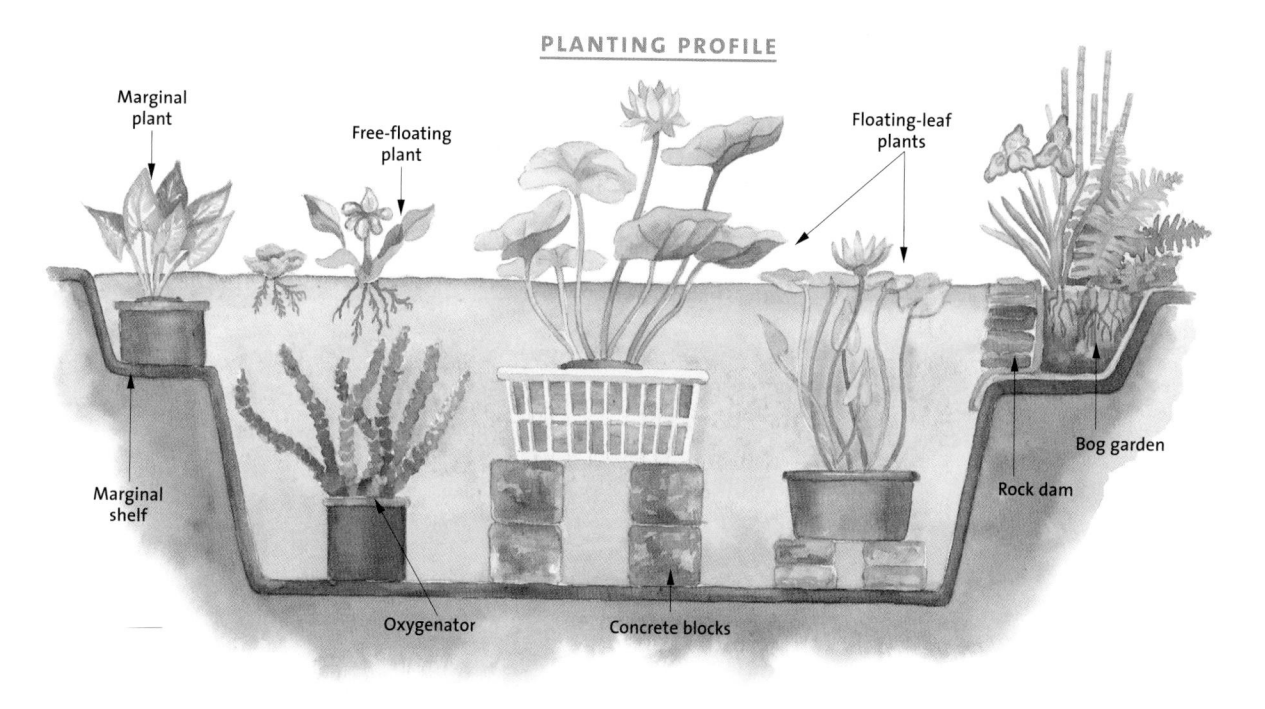

Marginal plant

Free-floating plant

Floating-leaf plants

Bog garden

Rock dam

Marginal shelf

Oxygenator

Concrete blocks

A Closer Look at Water Lilies

These flamboyant floating-leaf plants are the reason many gardeners build ponds. Bearing exquisite blooms over a long period, water lilies (*Nymphaea*) are the showpieces of any water garden. Even when the plant is out of bloom, the lily pads—the rounded, deeply notched floating leaves—are eye-catching.

Water lilies come in both hardy and tropical varieties. Hardy lilies bloom during daylight, opening about 10 a.m. and closing after sunset. Tropicals include both day- and night-blooming versions.

Hardy types are the easiest for a beginner and can overwinter in the pool. Tropicals, which are larger, more prolific bloomers, must be considered annuals in all but the balmiest climates. With some effort, however, they can be rescued and stored carefully in a greenhouse or other cozy spot.

Tropical lily 'Attraction'

Hardy lily 'Comanche'

Plant hardy water lilies from early spring through October in mild-winter areas. Although the tropicals can be grown in all areas, they shouldn't be planted until average daytime temperatures rise above 65 degrees. Hardy lilies flower as early as March, and tropicals can produce their first blooms in May.

Most water lilies require full sun—5 to 6 hours each day at minimum—for the flowers to open. If you have to build your pool in partial shade, choose a location that gets morning sun, or search out more shade-tolerant varieties.

Plant each lily in a container about 15 inches wide and 9 inches deep. Fill the container halfway with moist soil. Hold the plant in place while adding soil around the roots, firming it as you go. Bring the root crown even with or just above the soil.

Cover the soil with a 1- to 2-inch layer of coarse sand or fine gravel, then sink the pots in your pond. Allow 6 to 12 inches of water above the container; greater depth limits the amount of light that reaches the root crown. If your pond is too deep, elevate containers on blocks or bricks. Add small fish and oxygenating plants to minimize the growth of algae.

Starting about six months after planting, feed plants monthly with aquatic fertilizer tablets. One placed deep in the soil should be enough for each 15-inch-wide container.

goldfish and koi

KOI ARE BRED FOR THEIR COLORS AND PATTERNS, BUT THEY'RE ALSO QUITE FRIENDLY—EVEN GREGARIOUS. IN THIS CHAPTER, YOU'LL MEET KOI, GOLDFISH, AND SOME OTHER POND CRITTERS. THEN LEARN HOW TO DESIGN A FISH POND AND MAKE FISH FEEL AT HOME. GIVE FISH A TRY AND YOU'LL BE HOOKED.

MEET THE FISH

OPPOSITE: Goldfish drift dreamily in the shallow waters of this pebble-lined pond. Clear pond water allows you to enjoy your colorful fish.

WHAT'S A GARDEN POOL WITHOUT A SOFTLY GLEAMING SCHOOL OF KOI OR GOLDFISH, LAZILY SWIMMING IN THE SUN? With some basic care, fish can be quite comfortable in your garden. In this section, you'll meet the most common kinds of fish that are suitable for garden ponds. For additional help in choosing your goldfish or koi, see the drawings and descriptions on pages 126–129.

Goldfish

For many of us, goldfish evoke memories of small, sloshing fishbowls (or plastic bags) lugged home as prizes from county fairs—and despite our best intentions, the fish often died quickly. Why? As you'll learn, goldfish need plenty of oxygen and water that's chemically balanced. The classic fishbowl is one of the worst possible environments in both of these regards.

Goldfish have been bred for centuries as hobby fish. Consequently, there are countless types, and they are a good choice for a small pool. They're normally quite docile and can coexist with each other and with other types of fish their size, but don't expect them to be as outgoing and friendly as koi.

Young goldfish are much less expensive than their larger kin. Just make sure they're 2 to 4 inches long when you purchase them; smaller fish have a high mortality rate. In a large outdoor pond, some varieties of goldfish may reach up to 16 inches in length. It's common for goldfish to live three to four years, but in ideal conditions they can live up to 25 years.

Koi

Koi present a kaleidoscope of colors and patterns. These are just youngsters; in coming years, they could grow as long as 2 or 3 feet.

Koi become family pets, coming when called, taking food from outstretched fingers, even allowing themselves to be petted. These creatures outlive almost any other kind of pet, and they may even outlive their owners.

Japanese koi, or *nishikigoi,* aren't goldfish; they're colorful carp. Koi have two pairs of whiskers, called *barbels,* on the upper jaw, while goldfish do not. Breeders name koi for their colors. There are single-color, two-color, three-color, and multicolor varieties. For details on koi types and terms, see pages 126–127.

In temperate climates, koi can live more than 100 years, although their average life span is 20 to 50 years. Koi will grow a foot in their first two years, and then an inch or two per year up to their full length of 2 to 3 feet.

It's best for beginners to start with fish that aren't too young (they're weaker) or too old (they're very expensive). A koi club or knowledgeable dealer can help you start off on the right track.

DESIGNING A FISH POND

A FISH POND CAN BE ALMOST ANY SHAPE, THOUGH IT'S BEST TO LIMIT SHARP COR-NERS OR ROUGH EDGES so the fish don't injure themselves. Adequate depth is even more important. The pond should be no shallower than 18 inches; ideally it would be between 24 and 36 inches, or even deeper. The pond must also be large enough so the fish have room to swim freely. Figure on 1,000 gallons as the minimum for a koi pond—that translates to a pool roughly 10 feet long by 8 feet wide by 20 inches deep. Goldfish can survive in smaller spaces.

If your pool is for fish only, place it where it gets some shade. This is good for the fish and will help keep down algae formation—plus, fish colors tend to be richer and deeper in shade.

A garden pool that includes both plants and fish can provide endless enjoy-ment with a minimum amount of maintenance. The right mix and proportion of plants will oxygenate the water, shade it from the hot sun, and provide food for the fish. You will need to keep at least half the water surface free from plants, because fish need oxygen to survive. In turn, the proper number of fish will produce waste that provides most of the nutrients plants need.

Protect new plants in cages until they're well established, and add rocks on top of the soil in plant containers to keep fish from rooting. A separate marginal area for plants (see page 118) is best for pool owners devoted to both plants and fish.

Goldfish live comfortably in water ranging from 50 to 80 degrees, but they prefer the narrower range from 60 to 70 degrees. Koi don't mind a change in water temperature if it's gradual. There is less temperature fluctuation in deeper pools.

If you really want to enjoy your colorful fish, the pool water should be as clear as possible. Pool filters will keep the water clear; the best koi ponds often have biological filters and sometimes even a second, mechanical filter—typically, a pressurized-sand filter. But even pools with minimal or no fil-tration can be crystal clear. Water is balanced nat-urally, as discussed on page 131. For plumbing details, see pages 32–37.

Lush plants and fish share this pond. A rock dam defines a marginal planting pocket and keeps the koi from munching the plants for dessert.

ABOVE: This flagstone-ringed pond combines still planting pockets with plenty of aeration for fish, thanks to the small waterfall at one end. INSET: A plant island in the center of this pond provides cheery color while offering a haven from hungry koi.

POND FISH

KOI AND GOLDFISH ARE BY FAR THE MOST POPULAR CHOICES FOR WATER GARDENS. But keep in mind other, less obvious choices, such as the golden orfe, killifish, and stick-leback. Here's a closer look at them all.

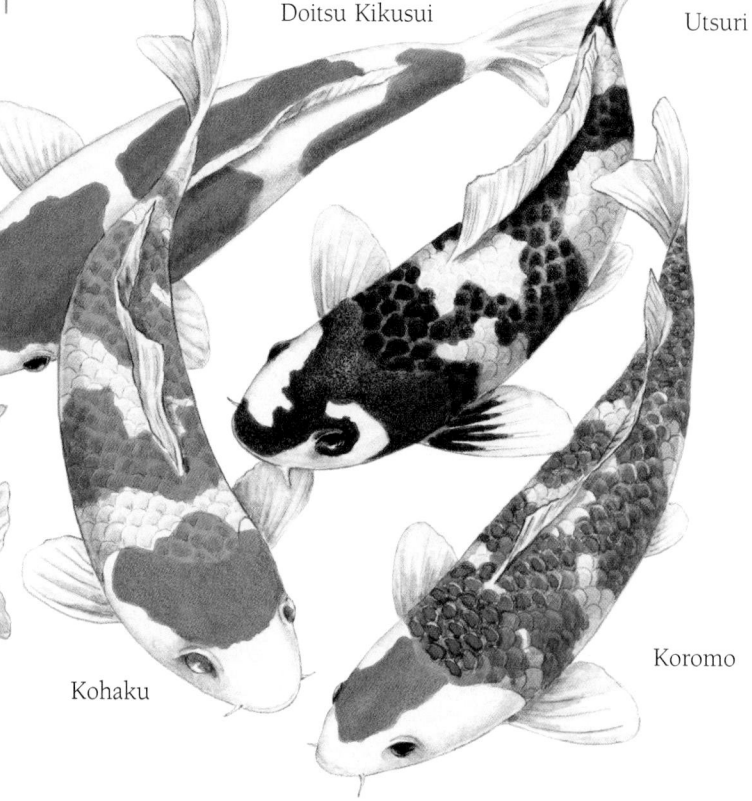

Doitsu Kikusui

Utsuri

Kohaku

Koromo

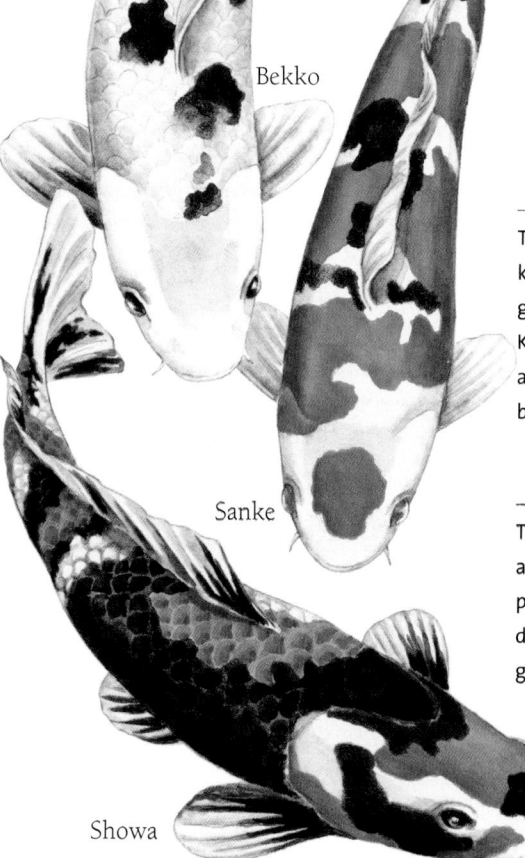

Bekko

Sanke

Showa

Koi Varieties

Kohaku

The most popular variety, this classic koi features red patches on a white background. Indicators of an exceptional Kohaku are a bright, uniform red (hi) color, a crisp-edged red pattern, a snow white background, and white fins.

Bekko

The most common type is a Shiro Bekko, a white fish with a black stepping-stone pattern down the back; the black usually does not extend to the head. Other background colors are red (Aka Bekko) and yellow (Ki Bekko), but these are rare.

Sanke

Also called Taisho Sanshoku, this white fish has red (hi) and black (sumi) markings. The black color should be deep and lacquerlike.

Showa

It is sometimes difficult to distinguish this koi from a Sanke, but here the fish is black with red and white markings.

Utsuri

The complete variety name for this black fish with markings of another color is Utsurimono. Shiro Utsuri has white as a contrasting color; Hi Utsuri has red; and Ki Utsuri, yellow. The black color usually extends onto the head.

Koromo

This one has the red-on-white coloring of a Kohaku, but with the blue, netlike scales of an Asagi (see facing page) on the red patches. Koromo means "robed," a reference to the brocadelike pattern.

Asagi

Its blue coloration is one of the natural carp colors. The entire back is covered in a net-like pattern of light blue or navy scales. Red or orange coloring appears on the flanks, fins, and tail. An unmarked, almost white head is the sign of a good specimen.

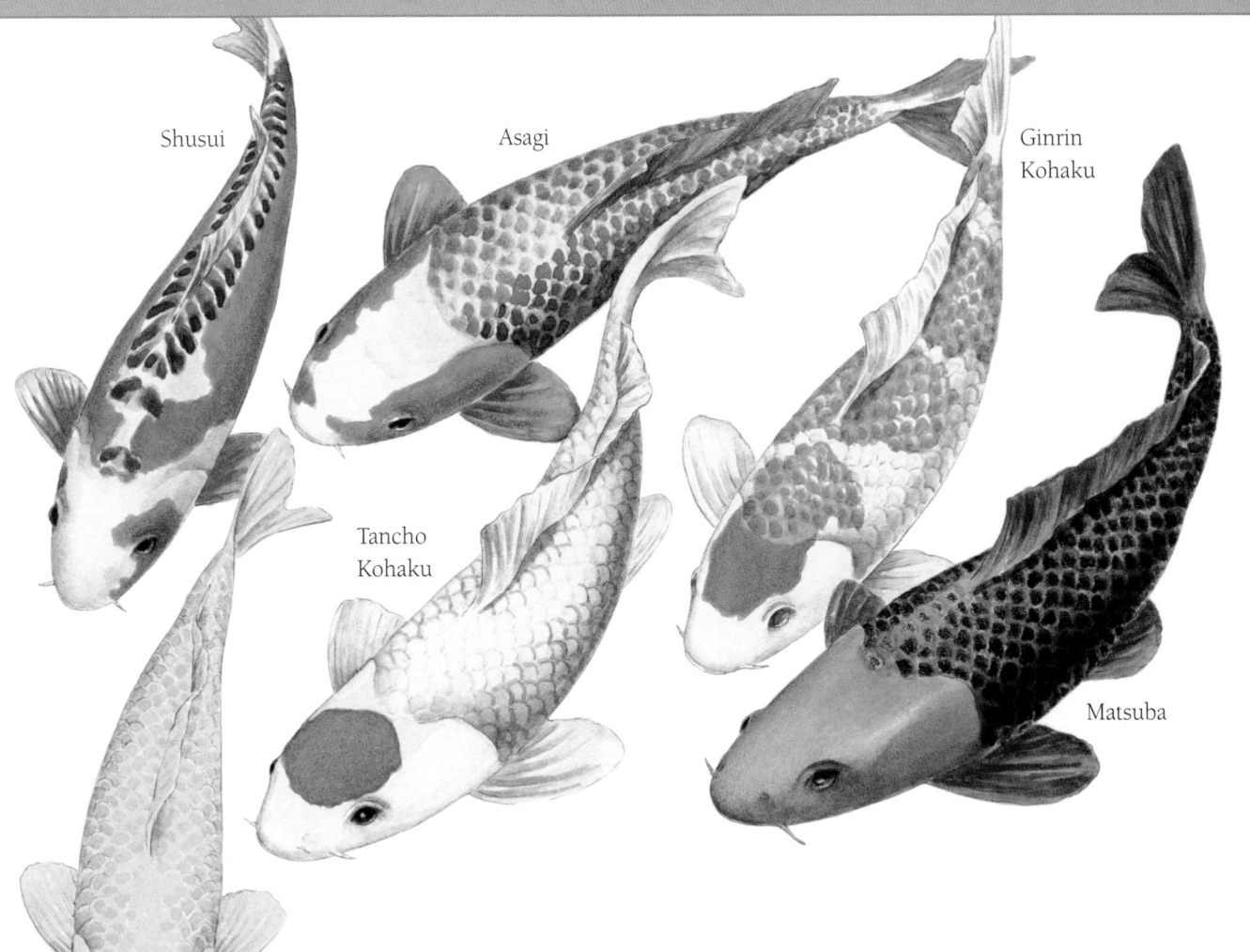

Shusui

Asagi

Ginrin Kohaku

Tancho Kohaku

Ogon

Matsuba

Koi Types within Varieties

Shusui

An Asagi with the scales of a Doitsu (see below right), this is a pale blue fish with dark metallic scales along the back and red on the sides and fins.

Ogon

Members of the Hikari group and the most recent variety of koi, Ogons have a metallic sheen throughout. Yamabuki Ogon is light yellow; Purachina Ogon, platinum; and Orenji Ogon, orange. Ogons with a single color are Hikarimono, and those with two or more are Hikarimoyo-mono. New color types are still being developed.

Tancho Kohaku

This is a Kohaku whose only red is a spot on its head. Ideally, the red should be intense, contained in as neat a circle as possible, and not extend to the eyes. The term Tancho may also be applied to other varieties, such as Tancho Sanke or Tancho Showa, provided that their only red is a spot on the head.

Matsuba

Koi of any color can be Matsubas if their scales have black along with the underlying color. Matsuba means "pinecone pattern."

Ginrin Kohaku

Koi with glittering scales are called Kinginrin, Ginrin, or just Gin. Shiny scales have been bred into almost all koi varieties; some look like diamonds or strings of pearls. Shown above, the typical red-and-white pattern of the Kohaku is covered in reflective scales.

Doitsu

Almost every koi variety is available as a Doitsu, which means "German scale"—the type was developed by crossing Japanese and German carp. The fish may have no scales at all ("leather carp") or a row of scales along the dorsal line. Kikusui (shown on the facing page) is a metallic Doitsu with a Kohaku pattern.

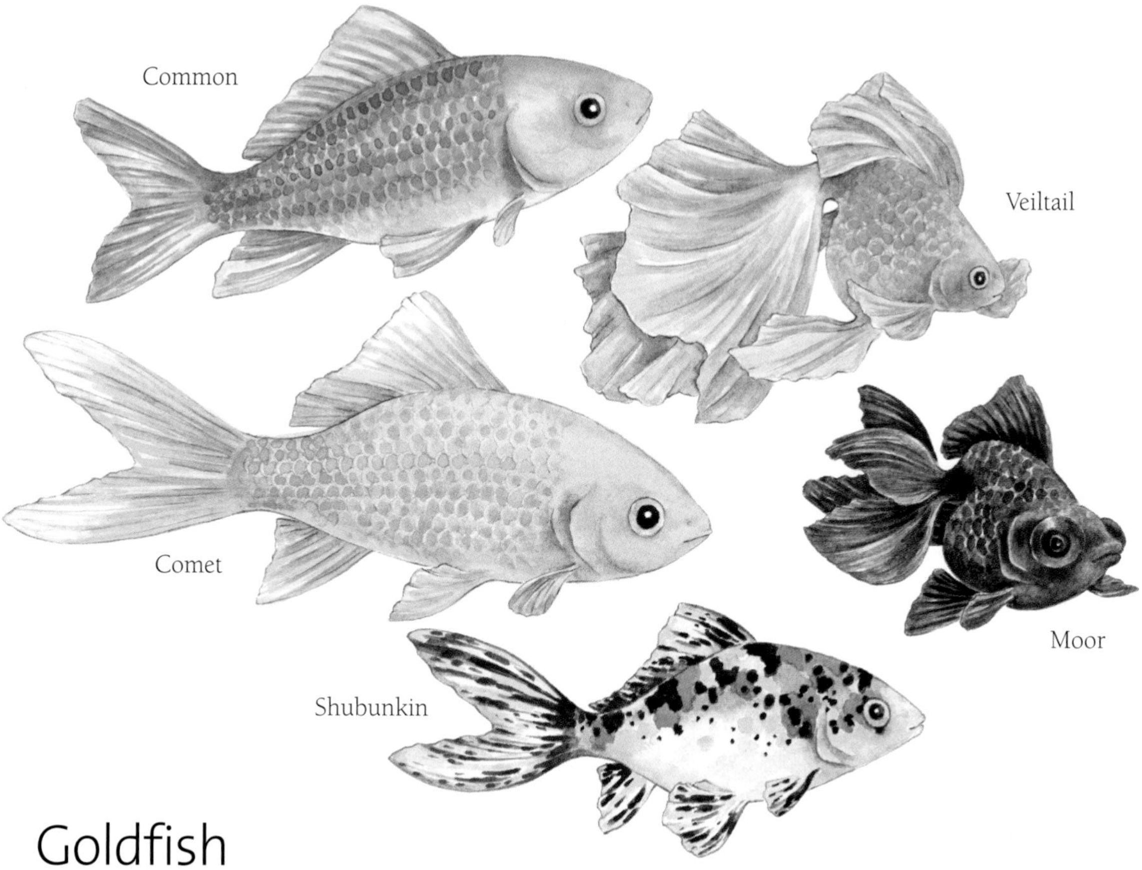

Common

Veiltail

Comet

Moor

Shubunkin

Goldfish Varieties

Common

This short-finned Chinese native is the original from which the fancy varieties were developed. An excellent swimmer and very hardy, it tolerates poorer water than do many other fish. Usually, Commons are a bright, shiny, red-orange, but some types are yellow or silver. They grow from 8 to 16 inches long.

Comet

This fish is similar to the Common, but the body is a "stretch" version, with larger fins all around and a much longer and more deeply forked tail. Fastest of all fancy goldfish, Comets are seen in yellow, orange, red, silver, and white forms. Sarassa is white with red markings; white with a red "cap" is Tancho. Comets grow from 8 to 16 inches long.

Shubunkin

There are three shapes of Shubunkin, all called Calico because of their coloring: pale blue flecked with red, orange, blue, black, and white. The Japanese Shubunkin shape is similar to that of a Comet; some have long, flowing tails. The London Shubunkin is shaped like the Common; and the Bristol Shubunkin is more rounded, with a big tail. All are fast swimmers and grow 6 to 8 inches long.

Fantail

A Chinese variety, the Fantail has an oval body with a double tail and fins much longer than a Common's. This graceful, slow-swimming type includes the Calico (scaleless, with Shubunkin-like colors) and the Japanese (golden orange); it may have normal or telescope (protruding) eyes. It grows from 6 to 8 inches long and must be brought indoors in cold weather.

Veiltail

This U.S. native with a round body and long, flowing tail and fins has a range of colors, but the most popular type is the multicolored Calico. The Telescope Veiltail has protruding eyes. All types grow from 6 to 8 inches long and must have indoor protection in cold weather.

Moor

From China comes the only truly black goldfish. Its small, chunky body grows only 4 to 8 inches long. The original Moor is a black version of a telescope-eyed goldfish, with a shape like that of the Fantail. The Veiltail Moor is a black form of the Veiltail. Both need to be kept indoors in cold weather.

Fantail

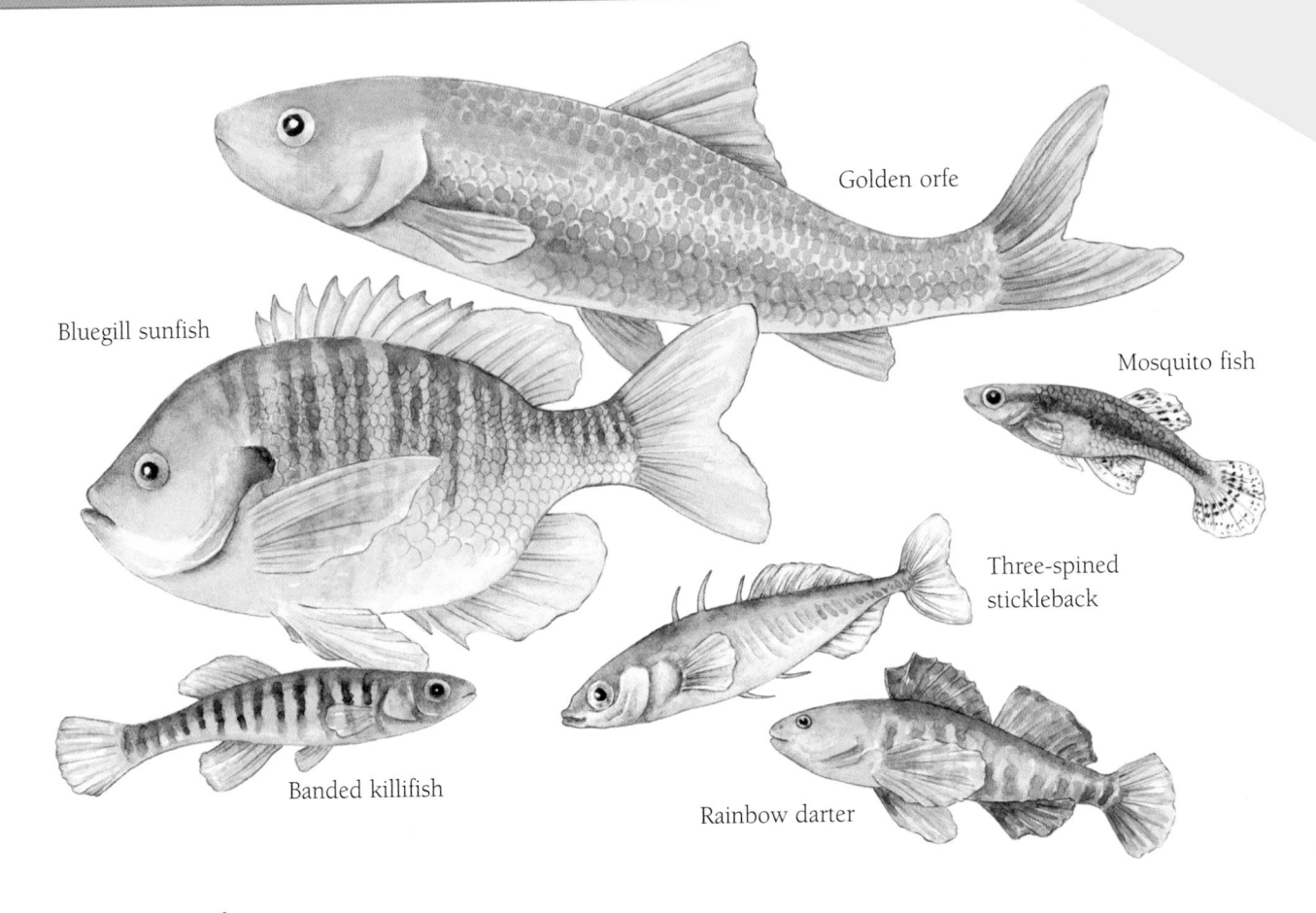

Golden orfe

Bluegill sunfish

Mosquito fish

Three-spined
stickleback

Banded killifish

Rainbow darter

Other
Pond Fish

Banded killifish

Native from South Carolina to Newfoundland
and inland along the St. Lawrence, the Great
Lakes, and the upper Mississippi, this fish
grows to about 3 inches long and lives about
3 years. It grazes at all pond levels. As a
schooling fish, it's best in a group of about 12.

Bluegill sunfish

These U.S. natives from east of the Rockies
grow to about 10 inches long and live about
10 years. The male builds the nest and guards
the eggs; introduce one male for every two or
three females. Like other territorial breeders,
sunfish may eat the eggs and fry of other
fish. They also eat insects, mollusks, and
crustaceans.

Golden orfe

This fast-swimming European native needs
a large pond, where it can reach 2 feet long
and live about 15 years. It prefers deep, well-
aerated water and eats zooplankton and fish
(or it can be fed the same diet as koi). This
schooling fish is best in groups of four or
five. A sensitive species, it will not survive if
exposed to chemicals in water.

Mosquito fish

Native from the Rio Grande to the Atlantic
Ocean and from Florida to Delaware, the
mosquito fish grows to 2 inches long and
lives 1 to 3 years. The females (with dark
spots on their sides) bear live young; their
diet is insects, small fish, and crustaceans.
Stock these schooling fish in groups of 5 to
50, depending on the pond size. They are
often available for free from local mosquito
control districts.

Rainbow darter

Native to fast-flowing streams from New
York to Minnesota and as far south as
Mississippi and Alabama, this fish does best
in streams or ponds with small waterfalls or
rapids. It grows to $2^{1}/_{2}$ inches long and lives
2 to 3 years, feeding on small insects and
plankton.

Three-spined stickleback

This fish is native from Hudson Bay to the
Atlantic coast and from Baffin Island to
southern Virginia; on the West coast, it's
found from Baja California to southern
Alaska. It grows to 3 inches long and lives
about 4 years. The male (which becomes blue
with a red belly during spawning season)
builds the nest and guards the eggs. Because
sticklebacks are territorial, they are best
limited to two couples per pond. They eat
insects, small fish, and crustaceans.

HOME, SWEET HOME

ONE RULE OF THUMB FOR STOCKING GOLDFISH OR KOI IN YOUR POND IS ROUGHLY **1** TO **2** INCHES OF FISH FOR every square foot of surface area. But a better formula is patience. Simply start off with a few fish and work your way up. If your fish are healthy, your filtering system is in top shape, and the water is well aerated, you can add new fish to your collection.

Lily pads fan out across the surface, adding drama while keeping the water cool for fish. Just don't cover more than 50 percent of the surface with plants, or fish may not get enough oxygen.

Balancing the Water

Fish need oxygen, just like land-based creatures; they absorb it from water passing through their gills. To ensure that they'll get enough air, the pond's surface area should be as great as possible. In addition, some aeration—in the form of a fountain or waterfall—is beneficial. A small air pump, designed for the purpose, can provide extra aeration in still ponds and keep beneficial bacteria alive if the filter pump fails.

A bigger problem is ammonia in the water. Fish respiration and other wastes produce ammonia, as do uneaten food and plant debris on the pool bottom.

Biological filtration is one way to deal with ammonia; mechanical filtration with zeolite as the medium is also touted by some experts. Natural filtration from plants such as water hyacinths can also be effective.

Other water problems include chlorine and chloramines. Chlorine, which is added to most municipal water supplies, is harmful to fish in large amounts; fortunately, it will dissipate in a few days if left standing. Chloramines (combinations of chlorine and ammonia) are very toxic; and as more and more water supplies are adding these to tap water, you'll have to take chemical steps to break them down.

Pool Ecology

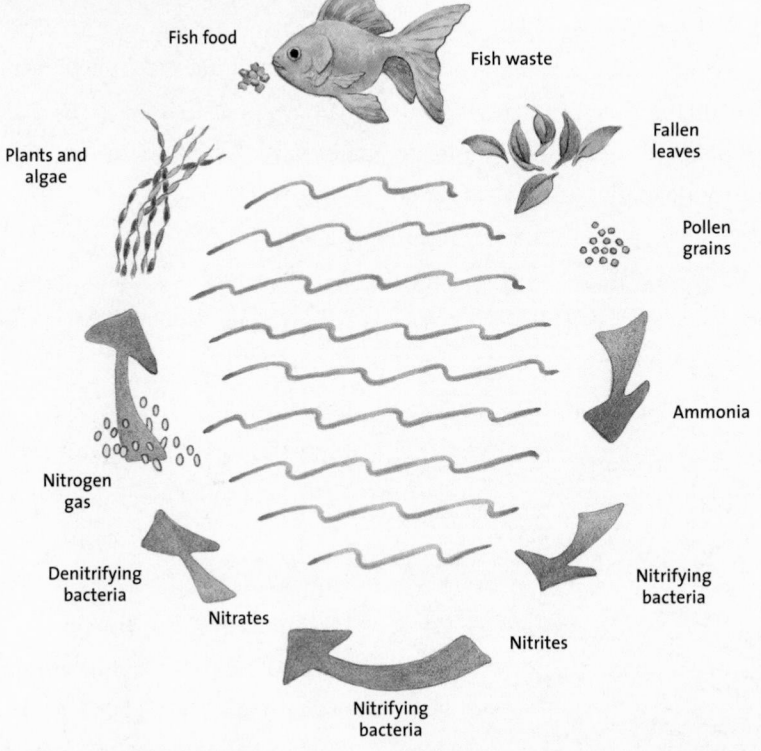

Fish food

Fish waste

Plants and algae

Fallen leaves

Pollen grains

Ammonia

Nitrogen gas

Denitrifying bacteria

Nitrates

Nitrifying bacteria

Nitrites

Nitrifying bacteria

Acting in direct competition for sunlight (on which algae thrive), floating plants such as water lilies keep water cool and clear. Small fish feed on algae and on insect larvae.

Owners of fish ponds have one additional concern: the buildup of toxic ammonia, which is excreted by fish. The key to grappling with ammonia lies in the *nitrogen cycle*, in which successive stages of beneficial bacteria break down ammonia into *nitrites*, then into *nitrates*, which are much less toxic to fish and which feed plants and algae—which in turn can nourish fish. Biological filters are designed to promote the growth of helpful bacteria. Aeration via a waterfall, fountain, or some other means helps provide critical oxygen both to bacteria and to their larger poolmates, the koi.

"Why is the water pea green, and what can I do about it?" Answering this common question requires a short lesson in pool ecology.

When water gardeners speak of a "balanced" pool, they're referring to its ecological balance. *Algae* is the villain in green; in a balanced pool, the growth of algae is controlled naturally. Floating plants, oxygenating plants, and some assorted pool critters are the good guys.

The pH (acidity) levels are also important. Whenever you're filling up a new pool, let it sit for a couple of weeks before introducing fish. Concrete pools must be cured; check the pH of the water with a pH testing kit. The best pH for a fish pond is between 7.2 and 8.5.

Proprietary products for getting your pool water in shape are available from pet stores and mail-order sources. Don't make frequent water changes in your fish pond—not only is it a waste of water, but you'll need to treat it constantly for chlorine, chloramines, and pH levels. Instead, top up with a little bit of fresh water as necessary.

For more details on balancing and maintaining your pond water, see "Water Quality" on page 136.

Chloramine treatment

Introducing Fish to the Pond

Late spring or early summer are great times to bring home new fish, but they can also be released during winter in mild climates. Most fish arrive in a plastic bag containing a small amount of water and a blast of pure oxygen. When transferring your fish to the pool, float the bag on the surface for at least 15 minutes, which lets the water temperature in the bag gradually adjust to match that in the pool. (If the day is warm and sunny, shade the bag with a towel.) Next, gently open the bag and let the pool water enter, then ease the fish into the pool. They'll probably take off and hide; gradually, over a period of days, they should begin to feed.

If you're introducing new fish into an established pond, many experts recommend that you place them in a quarantine pool, or separate tank, for up to three weeks. This will enable you to screen the fish for unusual actions or diseases. If a fish is sick, it can be treated before the entire pool is infected.

Before releasing fish into the pool, float them in their plastic bag on the water surface for at least 15 minutes to adjust them to the pool's temperature.

Feeding

Fish don't need to be fed if your pond is balanced, containing insects, algae, and a lot of water plants—all of which fish eat. But if your pond has few plants or if you enjoy the interaction, feed them—just don't overfeed them. Neither goldfish nor koi have stomachs for storing food, so they can only eat a small amount at a time; the surplus just fouls the water. A good rule is to give them only as much as they can eat in five minutes.

Goldfish and koi are omnivorous; they'll eat almost anything.

Scatter floating food pellets on the water to bring koi to the surface. Many koi owners say that interacting with their fish at feeding time is among the most rewarding aspects of raising them.

Packaged fish foods containing a balance of protein, carbohydrates, and vitamins meet their needs; some koi foods include spirulina (a high-protein algae) or carotene as "color enhancers." Floating pellet foods are best—they attract fish to the surface, so you can enjoy watching them, and any uneaten pellets can be netted and removed from the pond. Basic rations can be supplemented with worms, daphnia, brine shrimp, and ant eggs for special treats. Koi also like fresh vegetables, such as lettuce or peas.

As winter approaches and the water temperature dips, fish appetites decrease. At about 45 degrees, koi effectively begin to hibernate, living off body fat until spring and warmer water rouse them from dormancy.

Fish foods

Pond Protection

Raccoon

Once you've established your fish pond, you may find that your friends and neighbors aren't the only ones interested in the progress of your gold-fish or koi. Domestic explorers, such as the family cat or neighborhood basset hound—or wilder visitors, such as herons, raccoons, and even skunks—may drop by looking for a little fun or the proverbial free lunch. Any one of these can devastate a prized fish collection in a very short time.

How do you ward them off? Sufficient pond depth, of 24 inches or more, is a big help. Most mammals can't latch onto your fish while swimming; they must find solid footing in the pool. Overhanging pool borders and dense marginal plants provide fish with a temporary hiding place; so do hollowed-out "islands" made from wood or stones and covered with water plants.

A pond running beneath a deck, with a solid wall above the water and fish-sized openings below, is another option. Netting is the surest solution for marauding herons, though this is usually a less than satisfactory solution visually.

A fence made of electric wire, anchored to insulated posts and strung completely around the pond area, also is less than beautiful and can make pond access difficult—but it is effective if carefully installed; these low-voltage units are available from home centers and garden pool suppliers. At the high-tech end of the spectrum, you can install a motion-sensitive alarm, but be prepared for false alarms.

Heron

maintenance

A LITTLE HOUSEKEEPING WILL KEEP YOUR POND LOOK-
ING GREAT AND THE WATER CLEAN AND CLEAR. IN THIS
FINAL CHAPTER, YOU'LL LEARN HOW TO TEST YOUR
WATER AND SCRUB YOUR POOL, MAINTAIN PUMPS AND
FILTERS, FIND LEAKS AND PATCH HOLES, AND KEEP YOUR
PLANTS AND FISH HEALTHY AND HAPPY.

BASIC MAINTENANCE

ONCE YOUR GARDEN POOL IS INSTALLED, YOU'LL WANT TO EMBARK ON A TIMELY MAINTE-NANCE PROGRAM to keep it in top shape. You'll find that a seasonal rhythm develops naturally, as it does for other yard maintenance, so that caring for your water garden will become as routine as looking after a vegetable or flower patch.

Water Quality

The water in a garden pool should be clean, aerated, and chemically balanced. A variety of factors can affect water quality, including algae, pH, ammonia, and chlorine or chloramines.

The chief problem in most water features is an excess of algae, which turns the water green. In a pool or fountain without plants or fish, clean, clear water can be maintained with chemicals, as in a swimming pool. But in a water garden or fish pond, filtration is the ticket. A biological filter is most effective here—perhaps augmented by a UV clarifier (see page 35). Some biological filters now come with a UV unit built in. For a quick fix, consider a pond-cleaning product that adds beneficial bacteria to the mix.

Pond cleaner

Just as soil pH (potential hydrogen) affects your garden plants' growth, water pH determines whether your pond's inhabitants will thrive. Measure the pH of your pool water before introducing plants or fish, and on a regular basis thereafter. Low numbers indicate acidity; high numbers are alkaline. A healthy pool should maintain a pH between 6.5 and 9.5; if you have fish, the range should be 7.2 to 8.5.

Many easy-to-use pH testers are available in pool and pet supply stores. If your reading shows a problem, suppliers also carry products that raise or lower pH.

In addition to pH testing, check your fish pond for ammonia levels. In light of the nitrogen cycle (see "Pool Ecology" on page 131), concentrations of both ammonia and nitrites should be as low as possible. You can buy separate test kits to monitor just ammonia, or a multitest kit that measures both pH and ammonia. To alter ammonia, small water changes are necessary until the readings come down to acceptable levels.

pH treatment

pH testing kit

Both chlorine and chloramines are toxic to fish. Chlorine will dissipate out of standing water in a few days, but you'll need to take chemical steps if your water supply has chloramines added to it. For details, see pages 130–131.

Pool Cleaning

Keep the surface of your pool as clear as possible. Use a long-handled leaf skimmer or a large rake to remove surface debris. Remove dead plants or fish as needed, and keep filters flushed (see page 138).

Although a properly balanced pool should stay in working condition for long periods at a stretch, an occasional draining and cleaning may be required. Generally, fall and spring are the two best times for a pool-cleaning project. In fall, you can extract freshly fallen leaves before they rot on the bottom of the pool, robbing plants and fish of oxygen. Also, it's time to bring in tender water plants for the winter months and to trim back dead stems and leaves. But spring, when the water warms up, plant life takes off, and fish are once again active and feeding, is also a good time to clean. In fact, "spring cleaning" is an especially apt term for fish ponds, as that's the time that fish diseases tend to swing into high gear.

If you've installed a drain, it's easy to empty the pool. Otherwise, drain it with a pool pump, or use a hose as a siphon to drain the water to a nearby low-lying area.

If you have fish, lower the water partway down, then net the fish and move them to a holding tub filled with water from the pool. Shade the tub and use a pump for aeration. Drain the rest of the water from the pool and remove plants.

Carefully inspect the pool shell or liner, especially if you suspect leaks. This is the time, of course, to correct any problems (see "Pool Repairs" on page 139).

To clean pool walls or a waterfall, simply spray them with a strong jet from your garden hose, then drain the pool once more before refilling it. Use restraint when cleaning—strong scrubbing or scraping can remove all beneficial bacteria from the pool.

Rake up any debris from the bottom of the pond, being careful not to damage the pool liner. Use a wet/dry vacuum to suck up the remaining muck left behind.

Refill the pool, adding a water conditioner if your water contains chlorine or chloramines. Replace the plants, but wait until the temperature matches that in the holding tub before reintroducing fish.

Leaf skimmer

Spray nozzle

Wet/dry vacuum

The pool filter and any screens should be lifted out and rinsed monthly. About twice a year, give the filter and pump a thorough cleaning and check for wear.

Maintaining Pumps and Filters

The instructions for your pump or filter should outline the maintenance the equipment requires. When water in a stream or waterfall is moving more slowly than is normal, the pump may be in trouble. First, check the screen and any prefilter. For a submersible pump, unplug the power cord and lift the pump to remove debris stuck in the screen. Also check the intake (shown below), which is usually held on by a few screws. Clean both it and the impeller with a strong jet of water, and then reassemble the pieces.

For external pumps, you'll usually only need to clean out the leaf basket, which is designed to trap debris before it can damage the pump. To remove the basket, shut off the pump; if the pump is below water level, turn off any valves. Then take off the cover, lift out the basket, and either clean or replace it.

To clean a cartridge filter, just remove the cartridge and hose it off, directing the water at an angle to remove the dirt and let it run off. Return cartridge to housing, replace the cover, seal it, and restart the system.

A biological filter's media bed requires a light raking about once a month to remove accumulated debris. About twice a year, you'll also need to either vacuum or backflush the system to get rid of excess sludge and sediment.

SUBMERSIBLE PUMP

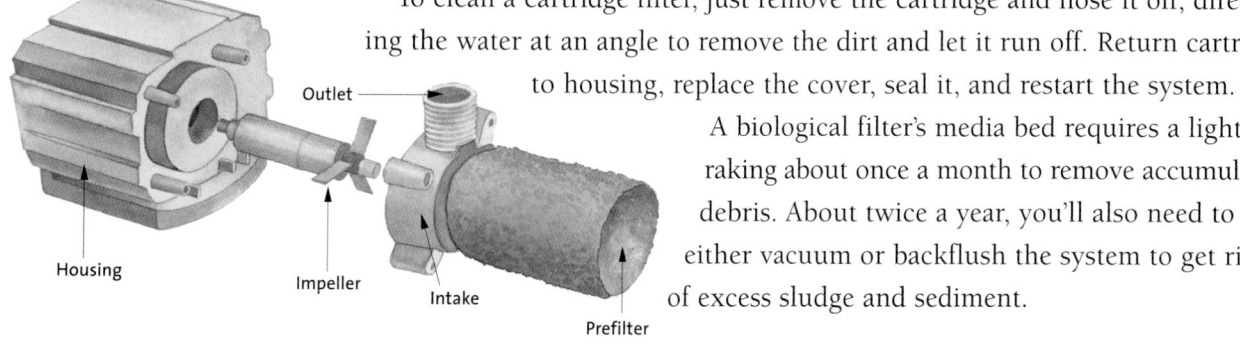

Housing

Outlet

Impeller

Intake

Prefilter

Pool Repairs

Whatever material your garden pool is made of, it may eventually tear or crack. The clue to a leak is the water level dropping faster than it normally would from evaporation. Fortunately, tears and cracks can be repaired (see the photos at right and below). The trick is finding them.

Before you start checking the pond itself, follow the routes of the water pipes to and from the pond to make sure that all connections are tight. The problem could simply be a leaking pipe or pipe connection.

Next, determine whether there really is a leak or if water from a stream or waterfall might be splashing out of the pool. If you see a lot of pooled water, or even just moisture, reduce the flow for 24 hours to see if the water level still drops.

Another diagnostic trick is to reroute the water through a large flexible hose so that it bypasses any streambed or waterfall. Mark the pond's water level and leave the pump running for 24 hours. If the level remains stable, the leak is in the stream or waterfall.

If none of the above is the problem, then you have to inspect the pool. If you have glued two liner pieces together (a practice many pool experts discourage), the leak is probably at this junction.

If you allow the water level to drop instead of refilling the pool, you'll eventually identify the level at which the leak is situated—that is, wherever the water remains for several days. Then it's a matter of cleaning and carefully inspecting the pool just above the water line in hopes of finding the problem.

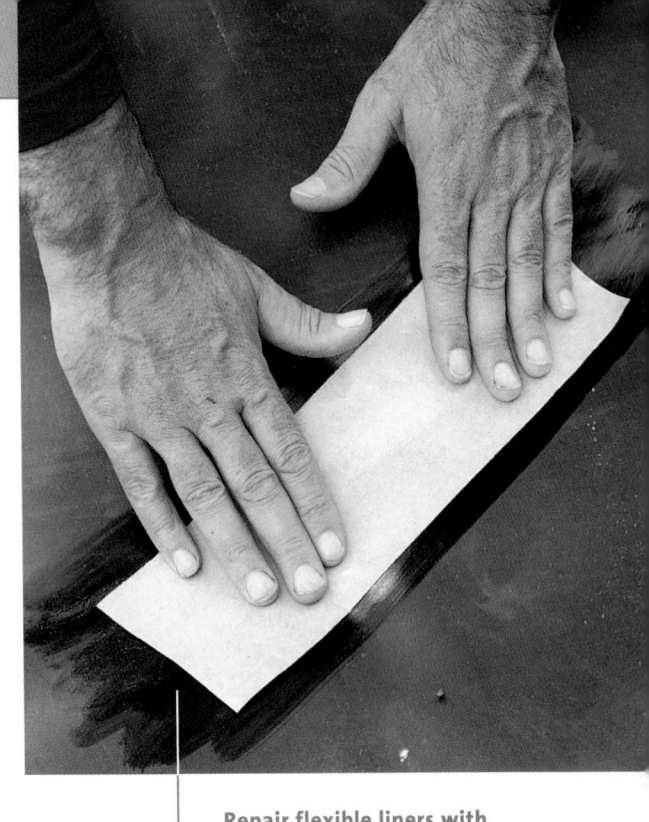

Repair flexible liners with seam tape or scraps of the original liner, plus an appropriate repair glue (ask your liner supplier for advice). First clean around the tear and sand the surface lightly; clean again. Brush glue around the tear, then press the patch in place.

For concrete pools, first clean a wide swath around the crack and chip out any loose material. Then use a caulking gun (shown at left) to inject concrete patching. Finally, press the repair caulk into the crack and smooth it with a wet finger.

CARING FOR PLANTS & FISH

A HEALTHY WATER GARDEN IS A BAL-ANCED ECOSYSTEM in which plants, fish, and other pond life work in tandem with pumps and filters to foster clean, aerated water. The previous pages covered the mechanical basics; here are specific tips for tending to plants and fish.

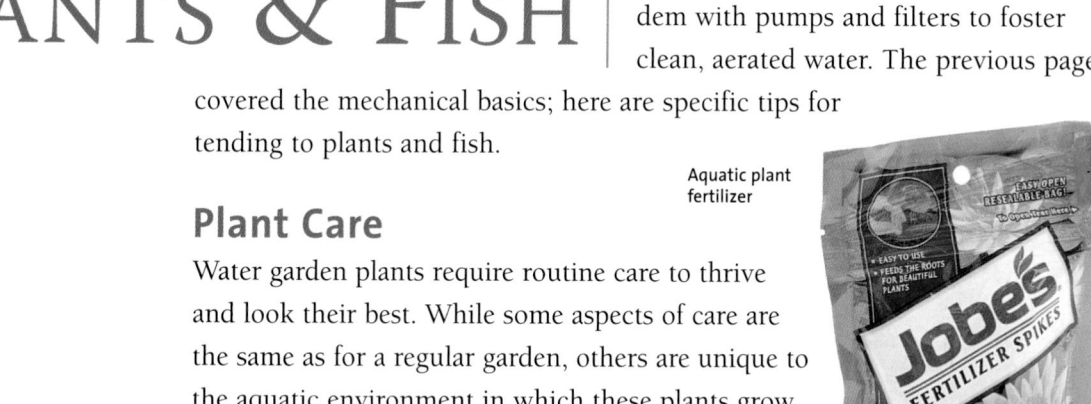

Aquatic plant fertilizer

Plant Care

Water garden plants require routine care to thrive and look their best. While some aspects of care are the same as for a regular garden, others are unique to the aquatic environment in which these plants grow.

Fertilize when planting. Additionally, you may choose to feed blooming plants monthly from mid-spring until about a month before the first expected frost. Fertilizers labeled for aquatic plants are safe for fish and other pond creatures, and they're low in nitrogen so they won't foster algae growth. Most water gardeners choose slow-release tablets (lasting 30 to 45 days), pushed deep into the potting soil to prevent them from leaking into the water.

Routinely trim any dead or diseased leaves and stems, as well as spent flowers. The best way to remove yellowed water lily leaves is to snap them off at the base of the stem. Lopping shears or pole pruners are convenient tools if you have to reach far out over the water. Some water gardeners simply wade into the pond to reach plants that are more than an arm's length away.

Be sure to prune back any plants whose growth is crowding into the pond or visually reducing its space. Even if they're not encroaching, grasses and sedges are among the perimeter plants that look better when cut back every year before new spring growth begins.

If free-floating plants spread too fast, they can take over just as weeds do. Use a net or rake to skim off excess plants. You may also need to thin out oxygenators to keep them from clogging the pond. Keep water lilies and many types of marginal plants in check by dividing them and discarding or giving away the excess.

Watch for plant pests and diseases. Aphids, a common water lily pest, can usually be controlled by washing the plants with a garden hose—or, if you have fish, they will soon consume the aphids. For

Two spading forks help divide the roots of a large clump of daylilies.

heavier infestations, apply an oil spray that's approved for aquatic plants; this will not adversely affect fish or plants. Rinse the plants with water about an hour after spraying.

BT *(Bacillus thuringiensis)* is an insecticide that is safe for use near pools and is effective for combating caterpillars and other pests that feed on your marginal plants. There is a variety of BT designed for eradicating mosquitoes, but if you have fish, you should have no problem with those insects.

First frost marks the time to protect your hardy water plants; lower them to the bottom of the pool, cover them with plastic, or—best of all—bring the containers indoors for the winter, keeping the plants warm and moist in a snug greenhouse.

Fish Care

Fish don't ask much, but a few basic procedures will keep them happy and healthy.

Spring is the time that water warms up and fish resume active feeding; it's also the time that fish diseases hit their stride. Therefore, spring is the best time for a thorough inspection of your fish, shell or liner, and pump and filter system.

Big, energetic fish like koi need elbow room, which a large pond like this provides. Fish suffer from overcrowding, but they can also be stressed by insufficient oxygen, temperature swings, and toxins in the water.

In winter, if your pond is 18 inches or deeper, you shouldn't have to worry about it freezing solid—especially if you keep a pump in operation. Lack of oxygen can be a problem, though; you may wish to run a pool de-icer that maintains a small hole to allow some exchange of air. An improvised pool cover—netting and straw, canvas awning material, plastic sheeting, or a sheet of glass or acrylic—can help maintain the water temperature. But, a small pool heater is the premier choice.

Of course, if you have a pond or tub garden with just a few goldfish, simply move them to warmer quarters when winter winds howl.

Fish diseases are due to either parasites, bacteria, or a fungus. To help you identify the problem, see the chart at right. A salt bath can help clear up many fish diseases; mix in marine salt at the rate of 8 pounds for every 1,000 gallons of pond water. Or treat isolated fish with a more concentrated bath: 3 ounces of dissolved salt per gallon for about 10 minutes.

Pet stores and mail-order sources sell proprietary medications for treating fish diseases. Standard treatments for parasites include trichlorfon and a mixture of malachite green and formalin. A variety of wide-spectrum antibiotics treat bacteria and fungus.

Don't try fish medications willy-nilly. Consult a veterinarian, koi expert, koi club, or textbook for help with any problem you don't understand. If you have a biological filter, be sure that any treatment you choose won't affect the bacteria in your filter media.

Fish Disease Reference Chart

DISEASE	TYPE	SYMPTOMS
Anchor worm	Parasite	Tiny twiglike worms, up to ½ inch in length, attach themselves to skin; twin egg sacs may be visible at end.
Cloudy eye	Nonspecific	As the name indicates, the symptom is a milky cloud over eyes; fish loses energy, appetite.
Columnarius (mouth fungus)	Bacteria	A bacteria, not a fungus as the name implies. Usually attacks head and mouth region. Contagious.
Dropsy (pinecone disease)	Bacteria	Scales stand out from body as on a pinecone, hence the name. Swollen abdomen is common. Usually fatal.
Fin rot/tail rot	Bacteria	Begins with light, foggy patches; progresses to bloody and rotted tail or fins. Indicative of unclean pond conditions.
Fish lice	Parasite	Lice are clear and flat, up to ¼ inch in diameter, hard to see without magnification; fish rub against pool sides and rocks in effort to remove lice.
Flukes (gill or skin)	Parasite	Gill flukes: Fish swim with jerky motion, mouth the surface, or face edges of pond as if exhausted. Skin flukes: Skin appears whitish; fish attempt to rub against objects in pond.
Fungus	Fungus	Cottony or woolly appearance on body or fins. Usually attacks previously injured or stressed fish. May appear whitish or even greenish (mixed with algae).
Ich (white spot)	Parasite	White spots like salt appear on body and fins; on close view, noodlelike parasites may be visible. Fish rub against objects. Often fatal if spots cover fish.
Oxygen depletion	Water condition	Fish hold mouth at surface, appear exhausted.
Ulcer (hole-in-the-side disease)	Bacteria	Open sores appear on body. Contagious, often fatal.

Acknowledgments

PHOTOGRAPHY CREDITS

Scott Atkinson: 39T; Maryellen Baker: 25TL; Christian Blok: 82B; James Boone: 86TR; Botanique Jardin de Montreal: 111TR; Paul Bousquet: 117; Paul Bowers: 125T; Marion Brenner: 18, 40T, 44, 45MR, 45BL, 46T, 46B, 47T, 47M, 47B, 49T, 49B, 62T, 80, 101T; Rob D. Brodman: 55R; Jack Coyier: 56; Crandall & Crandall: 113TR, 141; Robin B. Cushman: 8–9, 10T, 84T, 114MR, 122, 125B; Alan & Linda Detrick: 55TL, 82T, 111B, 114B; Andrew Drake: 25TR; Kerry A. Dressler: 110R, 111ML; Richard Felber: 15L; Derek Fell: 2B; Frank Gaglione: 94, 95T, 95M, 95B, 96T, 96M, 96B, 97TL, 97TR, 97MR, 97BR; Steven Gunther: 3L, 4ML, 59B, 61, 86L, 87B, 109; Jamie Hadley: 26, 27TL, 28T, 30L, 31B, 32L, 33B, 34T, 35MR, 36L4, 37TL, 37BM, 38TL, 39B, 40B, 41T, 41M1, 41M2, 41B, 48L, 62B, 64L, 64R, 65TL, 65TR, 65R2, 65R3, 67T, 67M, 72T, 73TR, 73MR, 73BR, 73BL, 89T, 89M, 116TL, 116ML, 116B, 118TL, 118L2, 118L3, 131B, 133TR, 136L, 136MR, 137T, 137M, 137B, 139R, 139BL, 140T, 140B; Jerry Harpur: 12; Marcus Harpur: 87TR, 106R; Philip Harvey: 24, 52L; Jim Henkens: 57; Saxon Holt: 14T, 102–103, 112BL, 113TM, 115B, 132R, 138T; Jean-Claude Hurni: 110L, 112TR, 112BR, 115TR, 132L; Andrea Jones: 23; Dency Kane: 115TL; Caroline Kopp: 7R; Linda Lamb: 98; Janet Loughrey: 25B, 54B, 81B, 113BR, 114T; Richard Maack: 13B; Allan Mandell: 14B, 53, 76–77, 79, 106L, 107, 134–135; Charles Mann: 1, 15TR, 20, 58T, 58B, 59T, 60, 78, 83T, 85, 100L, 104, 130; M.A.P.: N. et P. Miloulane: 84B, 143; David McDonald: 11L, 16T; E. Andrew McKinney: 29BR; Terrence Moore: 83B; Daniel Nadelbach: 86BR; Clive Nichols Garden Pictures: 21T; Norm Plate: 3R, 5, 10B, 11R, 16B, 17, 21B; Norman A. Plate: 27TR, 32R, 35TR, 35ML, 36L1, 36L2, 36L3, 36L5, 37TM, 37TR, 37R2, 37R3, 37R4, 37BL, 37BR, 42, 43TL, 43L2, 43MR, 43BR, 65BR, 68, 69TL, 69TR, 69ML, 69BR, 88L, 119L, 119R, 136BR; Lisa Romerein: 50–51; Eric Roth: 4T, 7L, 120–121, 123; Susan A. Roth: 113BL; Mark Rutherford: 38TR; Richard Shiell: 112TL; Perry D. Slocum: 111MR; courtesy of Southern Progress Corporation: 22; Jenny Speckels: 126, 127, 128T, 128B, 129; Thomas J. Story: 2T, 6, 19, 35BL, 54T, 70, 71TL, 71L2, 71L3, 71BR, 74, 75TL, 75TR, 75ML, 75BR, 92, 93TR, 93R2, 93R3, 93BR, 99TL, 99TR, 99ML, 99BR, 108; Tim Street-Porter: 13T; Catriona Tudor Erler: 55BL, 63B, 81T; Diedra Walpole: 52R; Judy White/GardenPhotos.com: 63T; Bob Wigand: 105; Tom Wyatt: 124

Chelsea 2001; 57: Paul Harris; 58T: Carrie Nimer Design; 59T: Scott Mayer Design; 59B: Mark Bartos and Tony Exeter of BEM Design Group, South Pasadena, CA; 60: Tom Beyer, Beyer Landscape Co., Lakewood, CO; 61: Steve Martino & Assoc., Phoenix, AZ (www.stevemartino.net); 62T: Bernard Trainor + Associates, Monterey, CA; 64L: Sun Studios; 65R3: The Urban Farmer Store; 65TL: Roger Reynolds; 65TR: Roger Reynolds; 67T: Roger Reynolds; 67M: Roger Reynolds; 82T: Cording Landscape Design; 83TR: Phil Hedrick design, Grizzly Landscaping; 83B: Greg Trutza; 84T: Kit & Fred Fulton; 85: Martin Moskow Design; 86L: Jeffrey Gordon Smith; 86BR: Gilda Meyer-Niehof, stylist; 87B: Mia Lehrer, Mia Lehrer + Assoc., Los Angeles; 89T: The Urban Farmer Store; 89M: The Urban Farmer Store; 92L: Kirk Samis of Pondsaway, Barbara Jackel and Kurt Christiansen of Christiansen Assoc. Organic Gardens and Design; 98: Gay Bonorden Gray, Mountain View, CA; 102BL: Gerald Ouellette of G & O Landscaping, Sherwood, OR; 108: Gerald Ouellette of G & O Landscaping, Sherwood, OR; 125T: Jim Sandel, Landscape Architect; 134–135: Ilga Jansons & Mike Dryfoos, Kenmore, WA

DESIGN CREDITS

1: Carlotta from Paradise; 2T: Jim Robinson; 3L: Michelle Comeau; 3R: Kathleen Ferguson; 4ML: Sunshine Greenery, Los Angeles; 5: Rick Conger, Conger Construction; 6: John DeCamara, Zia Scapes, and Beth Rekow, Rekow Designs; 7R: David LeRoy, Santa Cruz, CA and David Warren, Oakland, CA; 8–9: Phyllis & Richard Null Design, Eugene, OR; 10T: Steelman & Sams, Eugene, OR; 10B: Matthew Henning and Heather Anderson, Henning-Anderson; 11L: George Little and David Lewis; 11R: Hendrikus Schraven, Issaquah, WA (www.hendrikus.com); 13B: Christy Ten Eyck; 14T: Michael Stusser and David Stucky; 14B: Jeff Glander, Tacoma, WA; 16B: Steve Sutherland, SSA Landscape Architects, Santa Cruz, CA; 16T: Enchanting Planting, Orinda, CA; 17: Huettl Thuilot Associates, Berkeley, CA; 20: Phil Hedrick design, Grizzly Landscaping; 21B: Hendrikus Schraven, Issaquah, WA (www.hendrikus.com); 21T: Duncan Heather; 25B: Darcy Daniels; 26: The Urban Farmer Store; 27TL: The Urban Farmer Store; 28T: The Urban Farmer Store; 32L: The Urban Farmer Store; 33B: The Urban Farmer Store; 35MR: The Urban Farmer Store; 37TL: The Urban Farmer Store; 37BM: The Urban Farmer Store; 38TL: The Urban Farmer Store; 40T: John Showers; 50–51: Elizabeth Robecheck, Clemens & Assoc., Santa Fe; 52R: Frank Perrino, Woodland Hills, CA and Laura Smith, Hollywood, CA; 53: John Pruden, Portland International Garden & Design, St. Helens, OR; 54T: Bernard Trainor + Associates, Monterey, CA; 55R: www.rainchains.com; 55TL: Marshalwick Horticultural Society,

INDEX

Page numbers in **boldface** type refer to photograph captions.